FAMILY DYNASTY
THE RESTORATION OF THE WORLD BEGINS AT HOME

SEAN MORRIS

TRUDIE MORRIS

With
MARCUS COSTANTINO

Family Dynasty: The Restoration of the World Begins at Home

Copyright © 2024 by Sean Morris

All rights reserved, including the right of reproduction in whole or in part in any form, except for brief quotations in printed reviews, without prior permission of the publisher.

All Scripture quotations, unless otherwise indicated are taken from The Holy Bible, New International Version®, NIV®. Copyright © 1973, 1978, 1984, 2011 by Biblica, Inc.® Used by permission. All rights reserved worldwide.

Scripture marked (NKJV) taken from the New King James Version®. Copyright © 1982 by Thomas Nelson. Used by permission. All rights reserved.

Requests for information should be directed to:

Family Dynasty, LLC

5960 W Parker Rd

Suite 278-211

Plano, TX 75093

info@familydynasty.co

ISBN: 978-0-578-28019-6 (paperback)

Cover design: Terry Dugan

Cover photo credit: Ty Downs on Upsplash

Interior design: Ben Wolf, Inc.

Editorial Team: Rob Bentz, Cristina Wright, and Amy Sinnott

First Printing: 2024

Printed in the United States of America

Train up a child in the way he should go; even when he is old, he will not depart from it.
~ Proverbs 22:6

To Dad and Mom:

I have been blessed by your coming to faith in Jesus and your embrace of family dynasty. I am inspired by your love and willingness to sacrifice for those around you; you have modeled and framed the foundation of the Morris Family Dynasty and our capacity to influence the world to the glory of God.

I love you, appreciate you, and embrace all that you model.

CONTENTS

Introduction	vii
1. The Original Family Planning	1
2. The Three Families	9
3. The Genesis of God's Design and Dominion	23
4. The Family's Source of Power	39
5. Did God Really Say…?	49
6. Family Dynasty Exercised is Dominion Enacted	65
7. Biblical Families	77
8. Family is the Vehicle for Good or Bad	97
9. Under the Dome	109
10. Dynastic Family by Design	121
11. Your Family's Mission	137
Epilogue: A Letter To "Nonfamily" Families	153
Appendix	161
Acknowledgments	163
About the Authors	165
Notes	167

INTRODUCTION

Story is where we came from. Story is where we're going. Story is what connects us and binds us to each other.

~ Jeff Goins, *Why I Believe in the Power of Story*

For the last century, many Christians in the western world—more aptly, Christian families—have abdicated their authority and are living as if they are kings and queens in exile.

We have given over the role of parenting to school boards, employment of our kids to corporate America, and governance of our communities to the leaders of this world, many of whom are stubbornly opposed to the will of God.

I am grateful for Peter Jackson's directorial magnum opus: his presentation of J.R.R. Tolkien's masterpiece *The Lord of the Rings*. Not one of us who read the books, or watched the movies, was left unmoved by Aragorn's triumphant return to the throne. The merriment of the people of Minas Tirith and those from cities near and far was a celebration of healing, as was the blossoming of the White Tree in the Court of the Fountain.

But I wonder, how much of the pain endured throughout middle earth in those years resulted from Aragorn's abdication of his rightful place on the throne of Gondor?

In the same way that Aragorn's family dynasty, the sons of Elendil, was crucial to the wellbeing of middle earth, so your family, empowered by God's *dunamis*—a miraculous and supernatural power— is vital to his plan to bless the world.

Often referred to as the *dominion mandate* (and in some circles the *cultural mandate*), God's words to the first couple, Adam and Eve, defined his intent for humanity: "God blessed them and said to them, 'Be fruitful and increase in number; fill the earth and subdue it. Rule over the fish in the sea and the birds in the sky and over every living creature that moves on the ground'" (Genesis 1:28).

> *From the very beginning, as time first began its methodical tick, God implemented his plan to bless the earth through family dynasty.*

This intention of will has never changed. It continues through the millennia and stands today as the primary will of God for his people. Every family has the inescapable duty to participate in the joy of administering his plan to bless the whole earth. How? By leveraging their family's multigenerational influence through the intentional development of a family purpose to follow God as one *oikos*, as one household, following God's intentional plan for the world.

The dominion mandate has five components:

1. It was **given to** Adam and Eve—the first couple—and, by extension, every married man and woman.
2. We are to be **fruitful** in all our endeavors—to the glory of God.
3. We are to **multiply**, creating biological children and disciples who will worship him.
4. We are to **fill the earth** as his chosen people, revealing the glory of God.
5. We are to work to **bring order** and hope to a waiting and wanting world.

INTRODUCTION

Just as every person and family carries the weight of brokenness that comes from sin, so too can every person and family be restored by God through faith in Jesus. In Christ, we are sons and daughters of the living God. In Christ, we are kings and queens, princes and princesses, and we have the authority and capacity to transform the world in which we live while we wait with expectation for the return of our King.

But we do not wait with clasped hands and fearful hearts, isolated from the world, and insulated from the brokenness by the windowless walls of our churches. We parent and wait. We work and wait. We govern and wait. We share the Gospel, disciple believers, serve the widows and orphans, and gather around the communion table for worship. This is all part of the plan. God the Father, in his grace, by the power of the Holy Spirit, through the work of Jesus Christ, has invited us to be ministers of the Gospel (Romans 15:16; 2 Corinthians 3:6); and we both enjoy and bear the responsibility of being these ministers of reconciliation and restoration (2 Corinthians 5:11-21).

Our role, with all of its simultaneous joys and sufferings, is directed by the author and perfector of life himself (Hebrews 12:2). We must understand God's role in our lives: He is both the director and the main character. He is the writer and the producer. God alone is good, and he alone is the source of all that is good. He, in humility, has given himself to us in love. This is the foundation of our identity: God's love.

William Shakespeare famously penned, "All the world's a stage, And all the men and women merely players; They have their exits and their entrances, And one man in his time plays many parts...."[1] This is, of course, the opening to his famous poem "All the World's a Stage" in which he diminishes the nature and role of men and women, stating we are mere players in this thing called life. Conversely, another of the British monarchy's great writers, C.S. Lewis, once wrote, "There are no ordinary people. You have never talked to a mere mortal. Nations, cultures, arts, civilization—these are mortal, and their life is to ours as the life of a gnat."[2] We are worthy of God's love because he chooses to love us. We belong to him because he created us. We are not ordinary. Our neighbors are not ordinary. Because our God is not ordinary.

When you read God's book, the Holy Scriptures, there are three great themes:

1. **The revelation of the existence of the kingdom of God.** Broadly speaking, the kingdom of God is the sovereign rule of God over all existence—natural and supernatural. The kingdom of God incorporates everything that has been, is, and will be (Psalm 103:19; Daniel 4:3; Romans 13:1). More specific to humanity, the kingdom of God is a spiritual and natural rule over the hearts and lives of followers of Jesus, those who, of our own will, submit to him and acknowledge his lordship in our lives (John 18:36; Matthew 4:17; John 3:5-7).
2. **The love of God demonstrated through his redemption of mankind.** Since the fall, when Adam and Eve believed the first deceitful words spoken to humanity, "Did God really say, 'You must not eat from any tree in the garden?'" (Genesis 3:1) and disobeyed God's command, all people have been stained by original sin. We have been exiled from the garden, lost the kingdom, and have been made to labor through this world with great toil and to bear the consequence of eternal separation from God, as "the wages of sin are death." But the story does not end there, for "the gift of God is eternal life in Christ Jesus our Lord" (Romans 6:23).
3. **The creation and purposing of families.** Adam and Eve were the beginning of the first family. God's chosen people, Israel, was a collective of tribes (multigenerational families). And today, Christian families gather as a community of believers—the church. Within God's church

are nuclear families, multigenerational families, and intergenerational dynastic families serving God in countless ways and with various means.

Embracing the Call

Throughout the coming pages, we will examine and embrace God's call to families to wield the blessing of dynasty to establish and maintain our dominion here on earth. For it is the family that is the primary vehicle God uses to carry out his desire to have his will done on earth as it is in heaven (Matthew 6:10). We will study the Scriptures and the heart of God and immerse ourselves in the grand story of the Bible so we can reframe our thinking and re-story our families to become the power on earth God intends them to be.

In many Christian circles, the family is seen as a means to the end —a very good means—namely to provide the best framework for raising true disciples of Jesus to fulfill and serve the mission of God, albeit, as individuals. When, in truth, the family is designed, equipped, and mandated to serve the mission of God, and to do it collectively.

But the family is under attack. Dynasty is under attack. Dominion is under attack. Why? Because the authority of God's kingdom threatens the evil one, and he, more than any of us, understands the fruit of the kingdom grows primarily through the influence of Christ-following dynastic families. But every kind of family—no matter how broken—can be restored by God's grace and become an integral part of God's grand story. Through faith in Christ, we are kings and queens with God-given authority here on earth; we must not wait any longer to exercise this authority.

As you begin your journey through this book, we will help you and your family re-story the narrative in which you live. We will help you embrace God's mandate, your mission, and your assignments as a family. You will gain the tools to reset the trajectory of your generation, shape and build your family dynasty, and grow a true spiritual legacy. This new alignment of your family's purpose to God's dominion mandate will change lives and transform communities around the world for years to come as we await the glorious return of King Jesus!

1
THE ORIGINAL FAMILY PLANNING

The family structure we've held up as the cultural ideal for the past half-century has been a catastrophe for many. It's time to figure out better ways to live together.

~ David Brooks, *The Atlantic*

Your family is crucial to the kingdom of God because families have always been the primary place of belonging in this world. That is not to say families are the only place we belong—we belong *to* our Lord and Savior Jesus Christ, and we belong *in* family. This is no small distinction. Jesus, in his prayer to his Father, reveals the heart of God. Speaking of his disciples (the first apostles), and all believers, Jesus prays, "My prayer is not for them alone [the disciples]. I pray also for those who will believe in me through their message, that all of them may be one, Father, just as you are in me and I am in you. May they also be in us so that the world may believe that you have sent me" (John 17:20-21).

All who are saved by Jesus Christ, belong to Jesus. Yet, we are not taken from this world at the moment of our salvation to be with

Jesus, but we remain in this world for a purpose. What is our purpose? The Westminster Shorter Catechism answers the age-old question: **What is the chief end of man?** *Man's chief end is to glorify God and to enjoy him forever.* Every Christian has a single purpose; we are to glorify the God who made us by believing in and obeying the one who saved us—Jesus. In his wisdom, God created humanity in his image to glorify him, be loved by him, and be his agents of good in this world. It has been this way since the very beginning.

God set something in motion in Genesis 1—his design and intent for Adam and Eve and their children—that he has never refuted, never retracted, and never replaced. It is this intent of God that is the key to bringing forth his will, goodness, and order here on earth, as it is in heaven. He created a vehicle designed to represent him as he is —Father, Son, and Holy Spirit. It would reveal his character and his nature. It would be the environment in which we human beings, created in his likeness, will carry his image. It is the place of belonging that enables us to grow into full maturity, that we may more and more carry and bring forth the kingdom's purpose and mandate on the earth. And how did God do all this? On the sixth day, he created Adam and Eve, and "God blessed them and said to them, 'Be fruitful and increase in number; fill the earth and subdue it. Rule over the fish in the sea and the birds in the sky and over every living creature that moves on the ground'" (Genesis 1:28). Author John Eldredge offers this perspective, "Like a foreman runs a ranch or like a skipper runs his ship. Better still, like a king rules a kingdom, God appoints us as the governors of his domain."[1] This is the dominion (or cultural) mandate.

Often mischaracterized as being given exclusively to Adam, this mandate to be **fruitful** in all our endeavors, **multiply** by creating biological children and disciples who will worship him, **fill the earth** with his glory, and **bring order** (subdue) and hope to a waiting and wanting world, was given to Adam and Eve: "God blessed *them* and said to *them...*" (emphasis added).

This command of God was given to the first family. In expressing his intent to Adam and Eve, he also expresses his delight. Being made in his image (Genesis 1:26-27), God imparts to us his character (who he is) and his conduct (what he does) and then invites us to wield this authority for his purposes.

King David, in one of his many moments of lyrical worship, echoed the heart of God recorded in the creation account when he wrote:

> *When I consider your heavens,*
> *the work of your fingers,*
> *the moon and the stars,*
> *which you have set in place,*
> *what is mankind that you are mindful of them,*
> *human beings that you care for them?*
> *You have made them a little lower than the angels*
> *and crowned them with glory and honor.*
> *You made them rulers over the works of your hands;*
> *you put everything under their feet:*
> *all flocks and herds,*
> *and the animals of wild,*
> *the birds in the sky,*
> *and the fish in the sea,*
> *all that swim the paths of the seas.*
> *(Psalm 8:3-8)*

David, captivated by the glory and majesty of God, acknowledged God's heart toward humanity and his intention that we share in his rule of the created order. Of all creation, we are God's masterpiece—his magnum opus. God is mindful of us. He cares for us. He crowns us with glory and honor. He has positioned us—through our family dynasties—to have dominion over the earth he has created, thus bringing about the fullness of his goodness to all people, everywhere, and all creation, everywhere.

And it is worth repeating that this mandate extended in Genesis 1, has never been replaced or retracted. In fact, it has been echoed and amplified! Following the worldwide flood, "God blessed Noah and his sons, saying to them, 'Be fruitful and increase in number and fill the earth. The fear and dread of you will fall on all the beasts of the earth, and on all the birds in the sky, on every creature that moves along the ground, and on all the fish in the sea; they are given into your hands. Everything that lives and moves about will be food for you. Just as I gave you the green plants, I now give you everything'" (Genesis 9:1-3). Notice again, God does not only bless the man but the family. In the same way that God blessed and commanded Adam and Eve in Genesis 1, he now blesses Noah and his sons. And God extends the realm of dominion to include all living creatures as a source of food.

Furthermore, one of the greatest manifestations of the dominion mandate is expressed in the Great Commission. Jesus told his disciples, and by extension, all Christians, "Therefore go and make disciples of all nations, baptizing them in the name of the Father and of the Son and of the Holy Spirit, and teaching them to obey everything I have commanded you. And surely I am with you always, to the very end of the age" (Matthew 28:19-20). Beyond simply having biological children whom we can teach to follow God, we are to actively birth spiritual children who will follow Jesus too. God is mindful of humanity, and he desires that we be involved in the process of reconciling all of creation to himself. From the first family in the Garden of Eden to the nation of Israel (which was a family of families) to the church (which is also a family of families), the author of life has given each of us—and our families—a profound part to play.

Have you ever wondered why Genesis starts with the creation of family and Revelation ends with the marriage supper of the Lamb? From beginning to end, Genesis to Revelation, creation to Christ's second coming, God celebrates marriage and family. And we humans, created in the image of God, have been granted authority to act like him and become like him. We are image-bearers empowered to bring order to the created world. We are followers of Jesus, filled with the Holy Spirit, being sanctified, and being made more and more like Jesus every day. We are part of the family of God, a family of families (the church), and, of course, our individual families. And it should be noted that we are adopted into the intergenerational triune nature of God himself.

I very much appreciate the power of story, and I marvel at the wit and wisdom of author and blogger Jeff Goins, who said, "Story is where we came from. Story is where we're going. Story is what connects us and binds us to each other." Each of us lives our own lives, but we do so within a much larger context that includes marriage, family, church, and God. We all have parents from whom we came. Most of us belong to and are part of an ongoing family, biological or otherwise. Some of us are believers and function within the body of Christ, the church. But all of us, without exception, are part of the grand story, which is the unfolding mystery of God being revealed through creation, in which we are image-bearers of his character and conduct.

Throughout this book, I will share the stories of families I know personally, and of those that we all know. In doing so, I present them as examples of families fulfilling their dominion mandate. It is not that we should compare our own stories to theirs, rather we should be inspired to follow their example. Being part of the larger story, it is invaluable that we live according to the humility and teaching of Paul who implores us: "Follow my example, as I follow the example of Christ" (1 Corinthians 11:1).

What is a family dynasty? Let's enjoy our first story . . .

The Moore Family

We need not only look in the historical record of the Old Testament books to observe God's glory: we can see the work of the Almighty now. The blessing of God is alive and well deep in the heart of Texas, where patriarch Terry Moore and family are a startup family dynasty standing on the shoulders of their grandparents and great-grandparents.

The Moore family was integral to the birth of the Dallas/Fort Worth metropolis; the family settled into the region and worked the land, of what is now north Dallas, for generations before selling nearly all of the family's real estate holdings decades ago. I have often visited Dallas/Fort Worth with Terry and his wife Susan, walking through neighborhoods built upon land their family once owned. We have also visited the family graveyard. One time, as Terry and Susan marveled at the region's landscape, they wondered aloud, "Why did our family ever sell off all this land?" It wasn't long after that Trudie and I stepped into the curiosity and started a decade-long journey, alongside the family, to understand the House of Moore.

Ever commercially-minded, the prior generations of the Moore family did indeed sell the land to aid the city in its growth, but they did so without an understanding of family dynasty and dominion. And in selling their land, they gave up their influence. But for the dynastic mindset of Terry and Susan, the story of the Moore family of Texas might be relegated to the dash between the dates carved into the gravestones.

One of the keys to creating influence in this world is private property ownership. And land and property ownership are inextricably connected to biblical dynasty: God gave land to Abram (Genesis 15:18). God gave the land of Canaan to Abraham and his offspring (Genesis 17:8; 50:24; Deuteronomy 6:10-11). God ordained the purchasing of land (Genesis 33:19; 47:20; 2 Samuel 24:24; Proverbs 31:16). And Jesus affirmed the understanding of land ownership and stewardship in explaining how he would be received by the world (Matthew 21:33-41). Today, many dynastic families own land and, by doing so, maintain or grow the strength of their influence in their cities.

While the faith of the Moore family traces back generations, it was not until these most recent decades that the Moores began to embrace their part in the dominion mandate of Genesis 1:28 and the promise given to Abraham that "through your offspring[2] all nations on earth will be blessed, because you have obeyed me" (Genesis 22:18). Today, they have regular family meetings where the children have a seat at the table (they are invited to express their opinions and influence decision-making), and the grandchildren are now becoming engaged. Together, they are making every effort to understand their family's kingdom purpose and act upon it in how they steward and manage their land.

Terry left the business world in 1987 to begin Sojourn Church,[3] but the business world never left the Moore family. Their son David, who is a commercial and real estate magnate in his own right, continues the family tradition of integrating commercial enterprise with Christian charity. Working together, the Moore family, Sojourn Church, and the business enterprises act as a monolith to bless the people of the region through significant philanthropy and transforming communities.[4]

Living in the Grand Story

Every person who has ever lived is part of the larger story of God. We are part of his creation.

Thinking of family, have you ever noticed how the Bible is one big grand story? Of course, you have! But have you ever noticed how in the middle of the supernatural battle—the fall of mankind and the redemption on the cross—there is a beautifully intricate story of one man woven throughout all of Scripture? The whole of the Bible is the story of

> *We have been made like him. And he intends that we act like him: but not only us, our families as well.*

Abraham's family. The Old Testament is the story of his biological ancestors (Genesis 1-11) and his descendants—the nation of Israel. And the New Testament is the story of his spiritual descendants—the church. We learn from the writings of the Apostle Paul, "those who have faith are children of Abraham" (Galatians 3:7), and "the promise comes by faith, so that it may be by grace and may be guaranteed to all Abraham's offspring—not only to those who are of the law but also to those who have the faith of Abraham. He is the father of us all" (Romans 4:16). All who are in Christ, by faith, are part of God's family!

All of our families (yes, even yours) are crucial to the kingdom of God. We are assigned the magnificent responsibility of stewarding all of creation for the glory of the King. Each of us, through our individual gifting, as part of our family dynasty, wields greater authority than we can begin to understand. And the authority is not given to the one, but the many.

∽

Reflection Questions

1. In the first chapter of the first book of the Bible, Genesis, God puts his plan in motion. After creating Adam and Eve, "God blessed them and said to them, 'Be fruitful and increase in number; fill the earth and subdue it. Rule over the fish in the sea and the birds in the sky and over every living creature that moves on the ground'" (Genesis 1:28). What are your initial thoughts of the responsibilities (be fruitful, multiply, fill the earth, bring order) that God gives his people? Explain.
2. These responsibilities are known as the dominion or cultural mandate. Consider how you have seen these responsibilities lived out in the life of your family. Have they been an important part of your life's goals? Why or why not?
3. Reflecting on how this mandate has never been replaced or retracted but has been echoed and amplified throughout Scripture, how might this shape the way you practice your faith? How do you lead your family? How do you serve in your church?

2
THE THREE FAMILIES

You don't choose your family. They are God's gift to you, as you are to them.

~Desmond Tutu

Now, having dipped our toes into the depths of God's purpose for humanity, we will continue to examine family dynasty and its role in the dominion mandate. And just as important as this objective theological exercise, in the coming pages, you will discover how vital your family dynasty is to the kingdom of God. With a sufficient biblical understanding of God's will for the world and your family, we will endeavor to embrace the story God has for you and your family.

But, as we begin, we want to do so with a little clarity and care. My fellow authors and I understand many people have strong feelings about their personal family stories, and the idea of family comes with a myriad of emotions. Few of us have an idyllic story worthy of a Norman Rockwell painting. Frankly, most of us see a lot of ourselves and our families in the darker side of many sitcoms. But God is at work. He is the God of redemption and reconciliation. And as we approach what your family is and can be, we will do so aware of the pain we carry from our own family dynamics and be sensitive to the unhealed wounds you may have from yours.

Additionally, we understand many people consider the words *dynasty* and *dominion* to have largely negative connotations. Some will conjure images in their minds having to do with global conspiracies and the alleged 200 families that rule the world. Others have fleeting thoughts of the spiritual realm and dark creatures. And some 80s television buffs will think of opulence in Texas. While we contend there is perhaps a sliver of the truth in all of these visions of dynasty, we must strive toward a biblical understanding of these words and the God who created them.

Thus, as we approach dynasty and dominion, we will do so rooted in the foundation of the Bible to convey truth as God states it and not how the lies of the world pervert it. To provide the overarching lens through which we will present family dynasty, it seems appropriate to reiterate the three great themes of Scripture as presented in the introduction.

The first is the revelation of the existence of the kingdom of God. Broadly speaking, the kingdom of God is the sovereign rule of God over all of existence—natural and supernatural. The kingdom of God incorporates everything that has been, is, and will be (Psalm 103:19; Daniel 4:3; Romans 13:1).

The second is the love of God, demonstrated through his capacity to redeem mankind. Since the fall, when Adam and Eve believed the first deceitful words spoken to humanity, "Did God really say, 'You must not eat from any tree in the garden?'" (Genesis 3:1), God has made himself known to Israel and now to all believers: "the gift of God is eternal life in Christ Jesus our Lord" (Romans 6:23).

And the third is the creation and purposing of families. Adam and Eve were the patriarch and matriarch of the first family, and Israel was a collective of tribes (multigenerational families). Today, families gather with other families in the community of believers, the church—the bride of Christ. There are nuclear families, multigenerational families, and intergenerational dynastic families serving God in countless ways and with various means.

A Family of Families Influencing the World

The church community is to reflect the actual construct of family. It is not to replace family; rather it is to be a spiritual gathering for those who are part of the body of Christ. It is to be the place where families gather around the communion table of God's grace, are edified through the teaching of God's Word, and where we express praise through various means of worship. The church is to be a place of family for all families—and for those who have no family.

The earliest churches, those referenced in the book of Acts and the New Testament letters, were—as some might call today—home churches. Why? Because they reflected the practice of the Jewish community of the day. When the people of Israel went to the synagogue, it was a gathering of at least ten men and their households. Did you catch that? And their households! Synagogues were the place of gathering for families, and so was the early (home) church. Church communities cannot be separated from family communities because they are intended to be a gathering of God's people and a support for families. But, first and foremost, the church must be a place of healing and restoration. That's why we must ensure our churches are not constructed and framed as orphanages.

More Than an Orphanage

While families provide a place to become who God intends for you to be, orphanages provide a room, a bed, and a meal. While families instruct children in wisdom, orphanages instruct children on rules and regulations. An orphanage is marked by its management construct and its ability to meet the needs of the orphans, repeatedly and consistently, regardless of where the orphan ends up. Conversely, God's church needs to meet the needs of families, helping them fulfill God's design.

For decades in America, our families, churches, and communities have been plagued by dysfunction and brokenness. Ever since Adam and Eve ate the forbidden fruit and Cain killed Able, the world has consisted of broken families. But, over the last one hundred years, we are growing increasingly destitute.

In his article, "The Nuclear Family was a Mistake," David Brooks writes, "The story of the family, once a dense cluster of many siblings and extended kin, is fragmenting into ever smaller and more fragile forms. The initial result of that fragmentation, the nuclear family, didn't seem so bad. But then, because the nuclear family is so brittle, the fragmentation continued. In many sectors of society, nuclear families fragmented into single-parent families, single-parent families into chaotic families or no families."[1]

It is the degradation of the family that is leading to the pain and suffering in our churches and communities. Poverty always follows broken families. Drugs and other coping mechanisms almost universally coexist with poverty.

Dynastic families that are intent on living out the cultural mandate and great commission through one family stretched throughout time are being degraded to generational families intent on simply leaving the next generation better off than they were, i.e., merely a legacy. These generational families that once focused their time, talents, and treasures on family businesses, personal legacy, and the future of the church, community, and country, are now being distracted by their home, and freshening up their "white picket fence." (Never mind their expensive hobbies, social media platforms, and catalogs of streaming channels.) They are living, and buying into a culture that claims we are mere individuals who must adhere to our personal authenticity and follow our dreams no matter the cost.

Nuclear families are being crushed by feminism, pornography, social agendas, abortion, and a multitude of ideologies rooted in unbiblical teachings from ungodly men and women that purport family to be an unnecessary and even racist construct of white-thinking European men.

Brooks further explains the negative social and political consequences of the ever-devolving idea of the ideal family:

We've made life freer for individuals and more unstable for families. We've made life better for adults but worse for children. We've moved from big, interconnected, and extended families, which helped protect the most vulnerable people in society from the shocks of life, to smaller, detached nuclear families (a married couple and their children), which give the most privileged people in society room to maximize their talents and expand their options. The shift from bigger and interconnected extended families to smaller and detached nuclear families ultimately led to a familial system that liberates the rich and ravages the working-class and the poor.[2]

Only those who benefit from the destruction of families continue to perpetuate the supposed preeminence of the individual. And many who hold positions of national influence and power do exactly that. Why? Because, in most cases, absolute power corrupts absolutely. And when, in a society, religion and self-government are replaced by secular humanism and big government, the positive impact of families is greatly diminished. Because, for the most part, they cease to exist.

Now, there might still be some dynastic families in the world. There is likely some truth to the claim that 200 families supposedly rule the world; if it is true, it is because they are dynastic families intent on wielding their authority. They may or may not abide by the dominion mandate of God, but their influence to practice Genesis 1:28 is unmistakable. But, by the grace of God and the power of his promise, we can undo the evil of the enemy. We can embrace our collective calling and uphold the mandate God has given to every family. Again, from the introduction, the dominion mandate has five components:

1. It was **given to** Adam and Eve—the first couple—and, by extension, every married man and woman.
2. We are to be **fruitful** in all our endeavors—to the glory of God.
3. We are to **multiply**, creating biological children and disciples who will worship him.

4. We are to **fill the earth** as his chosen people, revealing the glory of God.
5. We are to work to **bring order** and hope to a waiting and wanting world.

We can bring order and hope to our families. We can bring assurance and confidence to the church. We can bring truth and eternity to the world. And we can bring healing, restoration, and transformation to our communities!

This begins with your family. It advances with every Christ-centered family. And it culminates with Jesus, our Lord and Savior. He is our King, ruling over us. And he is our Savior, giving us eternal life.

Names Matter

Inherent in the birth, life, death, resurrection, and ascension of Jesus Christ is the manifestation of every name of God throughout the Bible, "The Son is the radiance of God's glory and the exact representation of his being" (Hebrews 1:3a). Now, to understand the author's intent, it is necessary to understand the Scriptures he read.

From the beginning of time, humanity has been seeking God. The author of the book of Hebrews knew God and followed him by keeping the Abrahamic Covenant. He had access to the scrolls, which recorded the word of God to his people. And he understood God revealed his identity through the sharing of his names. "To know God's names is to experience his nature," writes author Tony Evans, "and that level of intimacy is reserved for those who humbly depend upon him."[3]

Throughout the Old Testament, God revealed himself, but only partially. This changed with Jesus, as God revealed his exact representation of being. Jesus, the Christ, is the manifestation of every name of God, "For in Christ all the fullness of the Deity lives in bodily form" (Colossians 2:9). Every name of God offers us a reflection of one element of who God is and his heart toward humanity. So, when we seek to understand who God is and what he desires of us, we must first look to Jesus. We do so as individuals who, by faith in Jesus, are reborn into the preeminent dynastic family—the Body of Christ, God's church.

Healing Broken Families

God is rewriting the stories of broken families just as he rewrote the story of earth through the cross. And just as he is bringing his children back to him, he is bringing prodigals back home. Knowing the end of the story as we do and understanding the heart of God as revealed in Jesus, we can begin the hard work of disbelieving the lies we hold onto and replacing them with the truth. This begins with an understanding of who God is—understanding the significance of his names—and who we are, having been made in his image.

As you begin to envision your broken family being restored, your marriage flourishing, and your children and grandchildren worshipping God with you, let your imagination run wild over the coming months and years. I want you to dream of the most remarkable picture of what your family looks like in the future. If 400 years from now is too far away, imagine three generations, or one hundred years. Imagine your grandchildren, great-grandchildren, and your great-great-grandchildren. What does your family look like in their generation? Are they living out God's mandate? Are they following Jesus? Are they making him known?

How do you see them positioned? Don't begin with the end in mind—begin at the end. Very big difference: because this will reframe your view. If you begin at the end, you can define (though not control) what happens between both. You can influence the present and the future. This mindset doesn't begin by starting to save today, wondering if your grandchildren will go to college. Instead, begin at the end. Consider how four generations from now your family is operating a small chain of grocery stores in your community. Or your great-great-granddaughter being a world-class surgeon. Or your great-great-grandson serving as a pastor and quoting your most recent sermon.

What you now have is a vision of your family dynasty. And if you have allowed yourself to dream, even for a moment, you have realized you are only part of the collective "we" that is necessary to materialize this vision. There are perhaps dozens of people involved in thousands of conversations with hundreds of consequential decisions. *This* is family dynasty! It is about the work we do in response to God's call on our lives to be fruitful, multiply, fill the earth, and bring order out of chaos—to cause his kingdom to break through into a waiting and wanting world.

God is at work. He is revealing himself to us page by page. And he asks us to seek him and his kingdom. We are told to pray, "Your kingdom come, your will be done, on earth, as it is in heaven" (Matthew 6:10). Notice Jesus didn't say it is God's will that heaven comes to earth, but rather God's kingdom and his will.

The contemporary church (and the whole world, for that matter) is enamored with the idea of heaven. We sing songs about the many rooms there. We imagine our grandparents looking down on us from heaven. We envision a place where there is no sickness, disease, crying, shame, guilt, or war. All of these amazing ideas describe the idea of heaven as we understand it, but heaven cannot be defined by our limited perspective of its attributes; it can only be defined by what makes it heaven.

Heaven is heaven for one single reason: Jesus Christ reigns supreme! And he does so for eternity. Heaven is not heaven because there's no crime. Heaven is not heaven because there's no pain. Heaven is not heaven because there's no need. Those are all of the benefits that result from the will of God being present in every moment of every day in Jesus Christ. But the real essence and reality of why heaven is heaven is because Jesus Christ reigns supreme. His will is one hundred percent manifested all the time. And that's the will of God: that all creation would submit to Jesus' lordship and worship him. Having been made in his image, God is making his people more and more like Jesus each day. And we are to make the earth a little more like heaven today, and in future generations, through our dynastic families!

Created for This

"Of the increase of His government and peace There will be no end" (Isaiah 9:7, ESV). On earth, as it is in heaven. It is the will of God that his will be done on earth as it is in heaven. The church does not debate how Jesus' government works, that God gives peace, or that eternity will last forever. But what we sometimes debate, and theologians wrestle with regularly, is when Jesus' government began or will begin.

Yet the truth remains—Jesus is the Lord. He is the Savior to all who believe, to those who have been redeemed by his blood. Jesus is Lord, not simply because he saved us, but because he is God. And the peace of God does not come as a result of his presence, once we get to heaven or even while we are here on earth, but it comes in full dependence upon his lordship. Peace is found in his lordship. Peace on earth results from his governance. It is the lordship of Jesus that redeems and transforms people's lives. It's the governance of God that empowers his kingdom, and the enemy knows it.

When the Godhead—Father, Son, and Spirit—partnered to create mankind, they did so differently than they had created the world. God *spoke* the world into being. But into man he breathed himself: "Then the LORD God formed a man from the dust of the ground and breathed into his nostrils the breath of life, and the man became a living being" (Genesis 2:7). We know "God created mankind in his own image, in the image of God he created them; male and female he created them" (Genesis 1:27). He breathed his life into us! He breathed his spirit, the essence of his own being, into humanity. God created mankind, both male and female.

We are apprentices on a journey to become like him, like our master, and we do so by learning to do what he is doing.

It all changed with the fall.

Adam and Eve had the capacity for dominion. Made in the likeness of God, they were stewards of all creation. They were given the garden, which was to be the pattern of ordering the world. They were given—like princes and princesses—the right to rule. And God has given this to you and me because, for those of us who are in Christ, we share in his kingdom rule, and we are princes and princesses of the Most High King.

> *With the breath of life in our lungs, the Lord of all creation mandated that we do his will by being fruitful in all our efforts.*

But what did Adam and Eve do? They surrendered to a lie of Satan.

But Jesus!

Christ's birth, life, death, resurrection, and ascension have purchased our inheritance back from death. This is the gospel! We have been restored to the place of Adam and Eve before the fall, just as God promised—saying to the serpent, "And I will put enmity between you and the woman, and between your offspring and hers; he will crush your head, and you will strike his heel" (Genesis 3:15).

From the very beginning, God would save the world through Jesus Christ, the offspring of Adam and Eve. Even in our sins, God is faithfully doing what he has always intended to do—redeem, reconcile, and restore his people to himself.

How does the enemy respond? He is undermining our identity: "'You will not certainly die,' the serpent said to the woman. 'For God knows that when you eat from it your eyes will be opened, and you will be like God, knowing good and evil'" (Genesis 3:4-5). He is undermining God's authority: "Did God really say, 'You must not eat from any tree in the garden?'" (Genesis 3:1b).

What are believers to do? We are to have the mind of Christ so we can know the will of God and follow his instructions (1 Corinthians 2:16).

But how does this happen? How can we, as individuals, families, churches, and communities, have the mind of Christ and know the will of God? How can we "be transformed by the renewing of [our minds]" so we can understand and follow God's will (Romans 12:2)? Thankfully, we do not have to search in the dark; God has made it plain from the beginning. It starts in the home with the multiplication of faith (part of the dominion mandate).

God instructs dads to train, not just raise, their children. God guides moms to convey wisdom, not indulge their children. We have been commanded to stand against the attacks and to regain the dominion we have naively and selfishly abdicated to Satan. He is undermining moms and dads and swapping them out with professors and celebrities. He is replacing prayer in schools with pornography in homes. He is busy defunding the police, demeaning justice by making it a social cause, convincing the world that biased interpretations of science are the author of the womb, and that elite leaders of the world are the saviors of the climate. He is busy convincing us to "exchange the truth about God for a lie, and worship and serve created things rather than the Creator" (Romans 1:25, tense changed).

But God.
But Dad.
But Mom.
But Family.
But Christians.
But the Church.

Beginning the Journey

As we launch into the journey of learning more about three great themes of Scripture, the kingdom of God, the love of God, and God's purpose in creating families, we do so by being mindful of the spiritual battle: "For our struggle is not against flesh and blood, but against the rulers, against the authorities, against the powers of this dark world and against the spiritual forces of evil in the heavenly realms" (Ephesians 6:12). Our holy resources are twofold: the armor of God is our weapon, and the dominion mandate is our strategy. And we leverage both under the authority of Christ who has already claimed our victory!

Yet, we are still at war. We battle with the forces of darkness in the spiritual realm. We battle with our culture. And, perhaps most significant, the battle we wage with ourselves. In his book *Becoming a King*, Morgan Snyder explains our plight and the purpose of Christians and churches.

> The Western worldview has done great harm to our understanding of authority. We live in a culture that deeply values self-sufficiency and is steeped in self-determination. Our culture cherishes the icon of the self-made man, and we spend most of our energy building, protecting, and preserving our personal kingdoms. Most of us have come to resent being under authority, because our experiences have confirmed the message that being under authority causes harm and constricts our liberty. Yet the kingdom of God is fundamentally different from the fallen kingdoms of this world. The kingdom of God prizes our willful consent to make the goodness, truth, and beauty of the true authority for which we were made under the care of God to be our ultimate refuge and seat of inextinguishable strength.[4]

I love how Snyder affirms our true authority, which corresponds with God's mandate that we "rule", and that this ruling is about goodness, truth, beauty, and liberty. This means that believers must unlearn the self-absorbed comfort-seeking we have been taught by the world, and replace it with a determined submission to the loving will of our King no matter the request.

We are at war because our King is at war. His kingdom, as unchangeable as the King, will stand forever. But, as sons and daughters of the King, we must take a stand in the fight for the lives of our families, our children, and our fellow citizens, whether they submit to the King right now or not.

Every family who chooses to move away from their own vanity to the glory of God must do so with the partnership of other families under the godly direction of the church. We cannot carry the full authority of Christ on our own, for the equipping of the saints is collective action; we share in the authority of Christ when we partake in the fellowship within the church.

What I am calling for is no less than a worldwide re-storying of families into family dynasties. I envision biblical families embracing their dominion mandate to be fruitful in all their endeavors, multiplying those who worship God, filling the earth with his glory, and bringing the lordship of Christ to the world.

Reflection Questions

1. As you consider your family—it's size, skills, connectedness, pains, story, and more—what must you do to refrain from comparing your family to others and instead embrace God's love and blessing of your family? How will you receive God's encouragement without negatively judging where you and your family are right now?
2. There are many ways that God demonstrates his love and commitment to his people. Which of the three ways summarized on page 10 has had the most impact on your faith journey?
3. We encourage you to "begin at the end" rather than simply having the end in mind regarding building your own dynastic family. Take a few moments to journal your "end."
4. In light of the ongoing threat that families are to Satan and his attacks in response, what lies does he continue to send your way? What does the Bible say about those lies?

3
THE GENESIS OF GOD'S DESIGN AND DOMINION

As God's image bearers in creation, we were intended to act as His representatives. We were designed, in a very real way, to show the world what God is like. So when God gave us the command to rule over the earth, the expectation was to do so in a way that reflected His character.

~ Aaron Armstrong, *The Gospel Project*

What would Adam and Eve and their family be doing today if they hadn't fallen? They would be enthusiastically joining God in his work of ordering the world! They would seek to be fruitful in all they do, multiply biologically and spiritually, and they would be filling the earth with God's glory. This is the work designated for them and us in the garden before the fall. This mandate is how God's will and purposes will be accomplished throughout the world.

Not long ago, I heard a sermon in which the pastor taught that this world belonged to the devil, and we should understand how his evil intent rules over and governs the Middle East. He also expressed that some of the people of this region of the world are the enemy of

God; I wanted to reach through my radio and slap him! While it is true that there is a spiritual battle that rages in the heavenly realm (2 Corinthians 10:3-5), and the prince of this world, Satan, has been given limited authority by God (John 14:30), "The earth is the Lord's, and everything in it, the world, and all who live in it" (Psalm 24:1). God has also said, "Everything under heaven belongs to me" (Job 41:11b).

There is a battle that rages, and we are mandated to participate in winning it: "For our struggle is not against flesh and blood, but against the rulers, against the authorities, against the powers of this dark world and against the spiritual forces of evil in the heavenly realms" (Ephesians 6:12). We all belong to God, having been created by him for his glory. And we bring glory to the name of God in the heavenly realms by bringing about his will on earth through fulfilling our dominion mandate.

It has been said that life imitates art. And for those of us who enjoy stories told visually, especially through movies and television, we have often wondered: does life imitate what we see on the big screen, or does Hollywood simply tell the stories of life the way it is? When we look at the world around us, it's easy to wonder: What's going on? And it's easier still for Christians to look at the church and ask a more significant question: Why does it seem as though the world and its morality are creeping into the church more and more with every passing year? Generation after generation of believers sense that our worldview and biblical values are under siege. Candidly, this is a church issue because whatever happens in the church will be manifested in the world. It's not the other way around. We carry his authority throughout the earth. We are his image-bearers in the world in which we live. The demise of the world always follows the disobedience of the Christian heart, the self-serving Christian family, and the disengaged Christian church.

For the last fifty years, coinciding with the advent of global technology, numerous well-intentioned spiritual leaders in both church and parachurch organizations have been building orphanages instead of building up families. Additionally, many moms and dads, influenced by strong cultural voices and wanting their children to be happy, are raising young adults who are motivated to perform. Instead of being fruitful for God, we are perpetuating the efforts of the world. Instead of multiplying by creating disciples—biological and spiritual sons and daughters—we are fostering an environment in which individuals follow their dreams at all costs.

Today, many in the church are creating a culture of spiritual individualism that is all about me, myself, and I—an unholy trinity. Why? Because we are trying to add Jesus as just another teacher, just another god. We are preaching the good news of the salvation of Christ without the better news of the lordship of Christ. (And we wonder why the world is in the state it's in.)

Instead of acknowledging and teaching the will of the Father, the Son, and the Holy Spirit—the One True God—we often spread the valuable (but often abused) idea of a personal calling as if somehow God's will for my life is all about *me*. It's not! This isn't biblical thinking. Far less important is one's personal, spiritual calling when compared with God's mandate to all humanity to be fruitful, multiply, fill the earth, bring order, and create disciples. The calling we often conflate with our personal mission is actually God's calling. It's his calling that he bestows on his people as a mandate. This is not just my opinion: it is the revelation of God through the apostle Paul. He wrote to the church in Ephesus:

> Therefore I also, after I heard of your faith in the Lord Jesus and your love for all the saints, do not cease to give thanks for you, making mention of you in my prayers: that the God of our Lord Jesus Christ, the Father of glory, may give to you the spirit of wisdom and revelation in the knowledge of Him, the eyes of your understanding being enlightened; that you may know what is the hope of **His calling**, what are the riches of the glory of His inheritance in the saints, and what *is* the exceeding greatness of His power toward us who believe, according to the working of His mighty power which He worked in Christ when He raised Him from the dead and seated Him at His right hand in the heavenly places, far above all principality and power and might and dominion, and every name that is named, not only in this age but

also in that which is to come. (Ephesians 1:15-21, NKJV, emphasis added)

Instead of seeking to influence the world as individuals, we should endeavor to do so as families in response to his calling. I am confident this will happen because God has willed it and created in us the capacity to do just that.

I find it interesting that, in some mysterious way, the world is watching. And not just the people of this world to whom we are witnesses but also the whole of creation—those in the spiritual realm, those here on earth, and all of creation (seemingly both animate and inanimate)—is watching.

> *My heart, my dream, and my passion are to see the restoration of dynastic households that carry forth the kingdom by birthing sons and daughters who will fill the earth with God's glory and bring order out of chaos.*

Paul wrote to the church in Rome, "I consider that our present sufferings are not worth comparing with the glory that will be revealed in us. The creation waits in eager expectation for the sons of God to be revealed. For the creation was subjected to frustration, not by its own choice, but by the will of the one who subjected it, in hope that the creation itself will be liberated from its bondage to decay and brought into the glorious freedom of the children of God" (Romans 8:18-21). Like the watchful eye of Mordor in J.R.R. Tolkien's Middle Earth, the world watches and waits in anticipation for the glory of God to be revealed through the sons and daughters of God, but this glory is not our glory; it is God's. We are in the middle of God's rule being brought about on earth—his lordship being acknowledged and embraced. This brings about the increasing revelation of his glory, not only in the next world but in this one.

One of the great understandings and subsequent teachings of the Protestant Reformation is the acknowledgment that the Bible teaches *Soli Deo Gloria*: to the glory of God alone. One of the five major tenets of the Reformation, often referred to as the Five Solas, this precept understands that the work of God is not just to the glory of God but to the glory of God *alone*. There is no glory for me or you. God's glory is his honor, splendor, dignity, and identity. It is who he is. It is part of the name of God. The name of identity, Yahweh, means, "I Am." God does not share his glory: "I am the Lord; that is My name! I will not give My glory to another" (Isaiah 42:8).

But what God does do is graciously share his will, his purposes, and his work with humanity. This is how he goes about restoring once-broken families—by engaging them in his glorious work! God will restore your family by re-storying your family in Jesus and making you part of his grand story that began in the Garden of Eden.

This dominion mandate given in Genesis 1, at the very beginning before the fall, is also about stewardship. God delegates authority to Adam and Eve to be caretakers of the garden. More than just asking them to clean their room, he tasks them with the responsibility and authority to change how things are, to make them even better. He gives them a plot of land and says, "Farm it!" He gives them animals and says, "Name them!" God gave the first family a mandate to wield his authority, and he has never revoked this charge to his people. And while so much of Christendom in America today focuses on the role of the church, it must be noted that God didn't rescind his mandate to the family and give it to the church; he amplified it through the church. Jonathan White of the Theopolis Institute summarizes it this way, "When Adam and Eve sinned and were expelled from the Garden, the dominion mandate did not go away. God did not 'move the goalposts.' The story of humanity's dominion over the world is still the grand narrative arc of this world. Man's sin and the necessity for salvation are the dramatic complication and perfection of that arc."[1]

Theologian N.T. Wright adds another layer of depth to this mandate. He uses an ancient cultural role to explain the role of families today, "God created humans in the beginning to be his vice rulers over the world. That is part, at least, of what it meant that humans were made 'in God's image.' The 'image' is like an angled mirror, reflecting God's wise and caring love into the world, bringing order and fruitfulness to the garden where humans were placed. That project . . . has never been rescinded."[2]

The Significance of the Church

There is a profound relationship between families and the church. Symbiotic. Powerful! The church helps restore families, and families undergird the church. Much like Old Testament Israel was a family of families, and so too is the church today. The mission of the church is to make disciples to the glory of God. The mission of the family is to bring glory to God by making disciples. But the most effective way to make disciples is in families because discipleship is caught, not just taught.

Still, the church is a place of worship and belonging for all believers. Old and young. Married and single. Engaged and widowed. Growing and stagnating. Believing and doubting. The church is the one place in this world where everyone who professes Jesus Christ as Lord and Savior can gather to love God and give him the glory he deserves. It is also the place for those who are curious about the truth claims of the Bible and those who need fellowship, meaning, and purpose. The church is the glory of Christ.

But before the formal church was created on earth, God created marriage—the first and highest human relationship. It is so because it is a prophetic picture of the union between Jesus and the church, his bride. And it is so because marriage is a picture of the intimacy of the Trinity, giving us a glimpse behind the spiritual veil into the nature and perfect love of the Father, Son, and Holy Spirit.

What is remarkable and often overlooked in the creation account is that God created men and women as equals. Equally worthy. Equally loved. Equally created in the image of God. And he blessed *them*! The blessing of Genesis is not to Adam and subsequently through Adam to Eve, but equally to Adam *and* Eve. They, and we, are to live alongside one another, not one over the other.

Before we continue, we want to say in the most caring way possible that we understand the pain that exists in many of the hearts and lives of men and women when they feel left on the outside, while everyone else is warming by the fire. Many stories have been told that echo the emptiness that is created by not feeling seen or heard.

Many people, whether by a show of hands or by a cry from the deepest part of their souls, lament, "But what about me?" Some of us have never been married or are now living without a spouse. Some have no children or a family that disowned them long ago. Where do we belong? Where is our dominion? Where is our dynasty? What is our life supposed to look like?

Oh, what joy we have in expressing to you that you *do* have a place to belong—in Jesus Christ! God is your Father. Jesus is your groom. And the Spirit is your companion. As God's own, united to him through faith in Christ, you are not alone. You are beloved. You are seen. You are favored. And you share in the glorious work that was first given to Adam and Eve and then finished in Christ. Through the fellowship of the Holy Spirit, you have countless moms and dads, brothers and sisters, grandparents and grandchildren, in his church.

God gave Adam and Eve, and subsequently all of God's children, dominion on earth. Within the context of the family, the husband and wife collectively carry and exercise the authority and dominion of God within the household. Within the context of the church, each follower of Christ, empowered by the work of the Holy Spirit, carries the authority and dominion of God. But it is clear that dominion is purposed to and is most effectively wielded in families.

Without God's blessing, we are incapable of anything. But with God's blessing, we have the capacity and a plan to achieve what God has willed. And because of the work of Christ, victory is secure! This is expressed in the three stages of the dominion mandate: (1) God's purpose, (2) the strategy, and (3) the victory. Let us now look more closely at the mandate:

God blessed them and said to them, "Be fruitful and increase in number; fill the earth and subdue it. Rule over the fish in the sea and the birds in the air and over every living creature that moves on the ground" (Genesis 1:28).

1. God's Purpose
God Blessed Them

When God blesses you, it's related to capacity. More faith. More financial resources to use for his kingdom work. More suffering that leads to hope. More of his presence. More of his lordship in your life. It's amazing! It is not about prosperity as falsely taught by many preachers today. There is no "name it and claim it" in the economy of God; there is only his blessing to us and our humble receiving of his loving-kindness.

God blessed Adam and Eve. He empowered them. He put them and their family on the fast track to being like him and doing his work of stewarding the garden and the earth and everything in it. (Well, mostly, but we'll get to that in a minute.) The blessing was and continues to be a gift from God. We cannot earn it. It comes to those of us who are called according to his purposes (Romans 8:28).

2. The Strategy
"Be Fruitful"

Having been made in the image of God, "For we are God's handiwork, created in Christ Jesus to do good works, which God prepared in advance for us to do" (Ephesians 2:10).

God blessed us because he made us and loves us. God blessed us because he made the world and loves it. God has a lot to say about the foolishness of laziness (the opposite of fruitfulness). God is a creator, an artist, a musician, a scientist, a teacher, a priest, a prophet, and a king! And, being made in his essence, we are too.

When we work—so long as it is moral—it is one of the many ways we worship God, right along with our giving, abiding, learning, singing, and serving.

Increase in Number

Then God says to multiply. As a family embarking on building a family dynasty, the family's capacity (blessing) is increased quantifiably. Family is the primary venue for increase. As Christians, we plant churches, start businesses, serve in nonprofits, work in government, teach in universities, and most significantly (as this is the context of this passage), create and perpetuate families. This is the primary purpose of the strategy—the actual key—to *be fruitful and increase in number*!

From a business perspective, we would consider this to be opening branches or franchises. But whatever it is, whatever we are to do, we should do it understanding that our mandate and mission is to bring forth the power of God's kingdom here on earth.

Fill the Earth

The word *earth* that is used here can be interpreted to mean *all spheres of influence*.[3] I believe God has a sphere of influence for every family, not just every individual, but primarily every family. Dynastic families are called to bring forth the kingdom within every aspect of life. In concert with other dynastic families, within the local church, your family and my family can bring glory to God through the working out of our faith in a world that desperately needs to experience the fruit of our labor. What is this fruit? Nothing less than the goodness of God! And while one family might see their mission as serving in the realm of education, another might know their purpose is to reshape government. (We'll look at this more in the next chapter.)

3. The Victory
Subdue It

I think the reason many Christians (and, I dare say, some of you who are reading this book) have a visceral, negative response to the idea of subduing is because we misunderstand its meaning. Too often, we see a dark version of it. In war, we subdue our enemies. In sports, we inflict our will upon others in pursuit of victory. In marriage, some husbands demand their wives submit to them in selfish ways.

Here, the idea of subduing is related to bringing order out of chaos, *not* the more common and misplaced interpretation of imposing one's will upon another. In fact, there is much to learn about subduing from war. If the wars in the Middle East have taught us anything, it is impossible to extend peace through submission, but only through biblical governance—that is, by transforming lives through holy influence.

The principle of leaven helps us see the power of not ruling over, but rather reigning in. Living in this world, as followers of Christ, we are to enact the will of God: "The kingdom of heaven is like leaven, which a woman took and hid in three measures of meal till it was all leavened" (Matthew 13:33 NKJV). We don't talk much about leaven these days as most of us simply buy our bread at the store instead of crafting it on the counter and baking it in the oven. So, it is worthwhile to note that leaven is an agent, such as yeast, that transforms its surroundings (and, in the case of yeast, causes the dough to rise). But leaven does not leaven itself. We have the transformational power to change the dough (or the culture) only when we are kneaded into it. This is the way it has been since the beginning. This parable clearly frames our understanding of dominion. It is about the one God and the many people. It is not about you or me, nor is it about your family or mine, but all families. It reveals that dynasty wielded must always be done with a posture of humility, a heart to serve, and intentionality to engage. God has purposed us to transform our communities; we must be willing.

When we reflect upon the mandate, we realize Adam and Eve were the only two people on earth. They were given the authority to rule over the fish of the sea, over the birds of the air, and over every living thing that moves on the earth (Genesis 1:28). They were told to exercise dominion and bring order to every realm but never to rule over people. Why? Because there is only one King. There is only one Ruler. And it's neither you nor me.

Mowing the Lawn

In the spring of 2021, when Trudie and I moved our family to West Virginia, we rented a plot of land just outside of Huntington. This was the first time in a long while that we had land we needed to care for, and it was the first time our teenage son Jayden was introduced to the idea of stewarding something other than just cleaning his room.

We had just enough untamed acreage to benefit from the use of a riding lawnmower. I decided it would be Jayden's responsibility to bring order out of the chaos of the weeds in the field: it would be his little realm of the kingdom to govern.

I instructed him on how to fill the lawnmower's tank with gas and introduced him to the machine's controls and my preferred method of mowing the lawn. I blessed Jayden with a kingdom, the tools, and the knowledge needed to subdue our land. I don't know if you've ever seen a teenager drive a golf cart or a car for the first time, but as I was watching Jayden on the lawnmower, experiencing his newfound freedom and power, I smiled along with him. With a little guidance, he did a great job of taming the land and exercising his governance. (It took him the better part of the day, but that may have been his choice.) We celebrated his good work and went on with the rest of our lives, which for Jayden mostly included school and basketball.

A couple of weeks later, I noticed the weeds were roaring back. I pointed out to Jayden that he was losing the battle, and the weeds were winning. He responded, "But I already mowed the lawn!"

I had given Jayden a piece of the kingdom to oversee. He had the authority to rule, and he loved the power but hadn't yet embraced the idea of dominion. He knew he had permission to cut the weeds, and he knew he could use a lawnmower whenever he needed to. And more importantly, he knew how to use the lawnmower safely and effectively. But he had not yet embraced the reality that he was responsible for maintaining the lawn and enacting true dominion.

It Starts with The Fall

Ever since Adam and Eve fell in the garden, there has been a divergence in humanity. Some acknowledge the kingdom authority of God, and others do not.

Christians are in a constant struggle between the call of the world and the call of Jesus. In this tension, we can learn the will of the Father and do it by abiding in Jesus, all the while still creating idols in our hearts. And God is gracious and patient as he suffers, waiting for us to fully surrender to him. We live both in the kingdom of God (the place God created, which has no boundaries) and under the kingdom of God (where we acknowledge his lordship over all aspects of our lives, the only one who has ultimate authority). Our dominion authority has been reclaimed by Christ!

Yet our world is filled with others who are lost in their own mini kingdoms. People who have yet to submit to the authority of God and are busy creating environments where they can seek to control man—something that was never permitted by God in the first place.

Because of the fall, there is sin in this world. And because of sin, there is confusion about our identity. Because of the whispers of the serpent, many are confused about Jesus; and some have set their hearts against God. And because we lost the garden, and thus the kingdom, man has been trying to get it back by building empires ever since.

Empire-building is always directed by an individualistic mindset. It's about me. I become the dictator. Sadly, this even happens in areas of God's dominion—like the church and many homes. This is why there is such a high level of spiritual abuse in some Christian communities. Without Jesus as our focus, the temptation is to build our own empires. Sometimes, even with Jesus, we pretend we want his will to be on earth as it is in heaven. Yet many times, our actions suggest otherwise.

In his book, *The Mission of God's People*, author Christopher J.H. Wright explains, "God is passing on to human hands a delegated form of God's own kingly authority over the whole of his creation . . . human dominion over the rest of creation is to be an exercise of kingship that reflects God's own kingship."[4]

When we make the shift, and truly understand that we are commanded by God to join him in his glorious work of reconciling the world to himself (2 Corinthians 5:18), we can be amazed at the level of influence, authority, and power God begins to release in us and through us! Like Jayden on his second go-around with the lawnmower, we already have it.

Family Dynasty Wielded is Dominion

Can you imagine the horror if Jesus released the full dimension of authority and power to us today? While we are still in our immaturity? I'm saying this not to any one person but to the collective body of Christ. Jesus, empowered by the Holy Spirit, submitted his life to the will of the Father. Jesus fulfilled the Old Testament law perfectly —every day and in every way. Jesus never gave into temptation, never hated, and never lusted. At any moment he could have called down a thousand angels, but Jesus never used his authority for his own glory. (This is what it means to be meek.) Today, it is the same power of God that raised Jesus from the dead that now dwells within us—the Holy Spirit.

As individuals, I don't believe we have the capacity to wield the authority of God in the fullness of his blessing because his blessing was given to Adam and Eve, the first family. His blessing was given to Noah and his sons, the only family after the flood. And now, Jesus has given his blessing to the church, a family of families, to be his witnesses to the ends of the earth.

Now, make no mistake about it; as individuals, we abide in Christ, by the power of the Holy Spirit, to the glory of the Father. But as dynastic families, we are blessed with the capacity to transform the church, communities, and the world through dominion (under his rulership). Restoration of the world begins at home.

Dynasty is an English word that originates from the Greek word *dynastia*, which is from the root *dunamis*. It means "a succession of rulers of the same line of descendants." Genesis 1 is about a line of descendants and their capacity to be fruitful, multiply, and fill the earth because of God's blessing.

The way we can bring order to the waiting and wanting world, transform governments for the glory of God, and educate children in the truth of natural law (God's law) is to slow down and create a plan to wield the power God has given to families.

Legacy is what we deposit in and leave for the generations; dynasty is what we build with the generations. Christian families need to move beyond legacy and build dynasty.

What's Your Lineage?

Again, I want you to consider your family lineage. Think about the history of your parents, grandparents, and great-grandparents. What are their faith stories? What were their professions? What hardships did they overcome? What influence might any of this have on you today?

Think about your children, grandchildren, and great-grandchildren. Are they part of your family or off building their own? What are they learning? How do you envision your family making a difference in the world 100 or 200 years from now?

When you think about influence in terms of centuries and generations and not merely years, it's far easier to take a deep breath when you realize Jesus has sustained the world since the very beginning. Yes, even on our days when we have done no work to hold the planet together—you can safely conclude there is no rush. You don't have to frantically react to every political, social, cultural, religious, or relational challenge. You can pause, pray, and petition God to reveal to you more of his plan and how you and your family fit into it. You can transcend applying bandages to our broken world and join in the process of restoring it. Time is on our side, not on Satan's. He knows that when Jesus returns, it all ends. We know that when Jesus returns, we all win.

Because we know we have been invited into the work of Christ, we can focus our energy not on what *I* must do but rather on what *we* must do, as one family, working across multiple generations. We can wield the unshakable, immovable, unchangeable power of the kingdom of God, going where God sends us, bringing his glory with us to the ends of the earth.

Now, whatever we build, it has to be dynastic. It's not about passing the baton to the next generation or saving the world's resources for future generations. It's about guiding all of the efforts of the entire family (across all current generations and framing the engagement of future generations) toward one collective, agreed-upon, God-given vision. Nuclear families are insufficient to impact the world for decades to come. Generational families are incapable of influencing the world for centuries to come. But dynastic families can influence the world now and in the coming millennia. (Should Jesus not return for another thousand years.) Why? Because dynasty is dependent upon the collective, collaborative, and simultaneous rule of all living generations embracing an intentional intergenerational work.

∼

Reflection Questions

1. Consider a few specific ways that you influence the world as a family, not just as individuals. Explain.

2. There are three stages of the dominion mandate: God's Purpose, the Strategy, and the Victory. Which one of these most resonates with you? Why?
3. Since Adam and Eve fell in the garden, man has been separated from God's original plan for humanity. How has the fall influenced your struggle to follow the call of God or the call of the world?
4. Take a few moments to reflect on your family lineage. Journal how their faith, professions, hardships, and victories have influenced your life.
5. How might living in a dynastic family change and/or influence the trajectory of the family that follows you? Explain.

4
THE FAMILY'S SOURCE OF POWER

The world is not moved by love or actions that are of human creation. And the church is not empowered to live differently from any other gathering of people without the Holy Spirit. But when believers live in the power of the Spirit, the evidence in their lives is supernatural. The church cannot help but be different, and the world cannot help but notice.

~ Francis Chan, The Forgotten God

We all know that in the British monarchy, in the House of Windsor, the ruling monarch runs the family. But have you ever noticed how? They engage every member of the family, all the way down to the youngest member. Each, as age and experience permits, is involved in the responsibility of serving within the monarchy. This is the secret of growing a family dynasty so you can wield the authority you have been given as men and women of God to rule over the earth. Get your kids involved! That is the key.

Now it is not just their involvement that makes a difference, but their embrace of your family's mandate, mission, and story. It is not just having a mandate and mission to enact, but of utmost importance is to receive the blessing of God that precedes it. How will this work for you and your family? The blessing comes in the form of the third member of the Godhead—the Holy Spirit.

Christ-centered dynastic families live out a kingdom purpose through the work of the Holy Spirit. Remember the Greek word dunamis is the root word from which the word dynasty is derived; in essence, dunamis refers to "strength, power, or ability." Jesus uses this word in Acts 1:8—just before his ascension to heaven—to give direction to his disciples on how to carry out the command they are being given: "But you will receive power when the Holy Spirit comes on you; and you will be my witnesses in Jerusalem, and in all Judea and Samaria, and to the ends of the earth."

The act of receiving dunamis is the act of embracing power and capacity. This is what a dynastic family is built upon. This is the power given to Adam and Eve before the dominion mandate in Genesis 1:28, and it is the blessing given to the disciples before they began their mission of being witnesses in Jerusalem, Judea, Samaria, and to the ends of the earth.

In the Greek language of the New Testament, there are nine words for power. The word dunamis is used infrequently in Scripture, and its use is limited to defining the power of God. Here are a few:

> "The angel answered, 'The Holy Spirit will come on you, and the **power** of the Most High will overshadow you. So the holy one to be born will be called the Son of God.'" (Luke 1:35)

> "But you will receive **power** when the Holy Spirit comes on you; and you will be my witnesses in Jerusalem, and in all Judea and Samaria, and to the ends of the earth." (Acts 1:8)

> "For since the creation of the world God's invisible qualities—his eternal **power** and divine nature—have been clearly seen, being understood from what has been made, so that people are without excuse." (Romans 1:20)

"Jews demand signs and Greeks look for wisdom, but we preach Christ crucified: a stumbling block to Jews and foolishness to Gentiles, but to those whom God has called, both Jews and Greeks, Christ the **power** of God and the wisdom of God." (1 Corinthians 1:22–24)

"But he said to me, 'My grace is sufficient for you, for my **power** is made perfect in weakness.' Therefore, I will boast all the more gladly about my weaknesses, so that Christ's **power** may rest on me." (2 Corinthians 12:9)

"Now to him who is able to do immeasurably more than all we ask or imagine, according to his **power** that is at work within us, to him be glory in the church and in Christ Jesus throughout all generations, for ever and ever! Amen." (Ephesians 3:20–21)

"His divine **power** has given us everything we need for a godly life through our knowledge of him who called us by his own glory and goodness." (2 Peter 1:3)

Learning and understanding how the power of God is rooted in his very essence—that we have been made in his likeness, that his life has been breathed into us, and that we are filled with the Holy Spirit—it can't help but reshape our thinking.

The spiritual gifts are expressions of the power of God for the people of God. And the people of God have the power of God for the sake of dominion. Where does dominion belong, first and foremost? In the family dynasty. Why in family dynasty? Because we are part of the family of God, which is generational in nature.

Looking back at the verses that reveal the word for *power*, we learn a lot about who God is and how he wields his own power.

In Luke 1:35, we learn of God's power in the miraculous birth of his son, Jesus.

In Acts 1:8, the people of God receive the power of the Holy Spirit to testify to a new generation of Christians.

In 1 Corinthians 1:22-24, Paul affirms that Jesus, the son of God, is the power and wisdom of the Father.

And in Ephesians 3:20-21, we are promised that the power of God will continue to work throughout the generations.

Again and again, the Bible proclaims the purpose and power of the generations!

As God's sons and daughters—part of the many generations of God through faith in his son, Jesus—we are now his representatives here on earth. We have the authority to build dynastic families to advance and expand the territory, wealth, rule, and governance of the kingdom of God. While we can't control the outcomes, we do have the capacity—rooted in the blessing of His Spirit—to order things, to bring justice to a lawless world. To strengthen the spiritual leadership of our homes. To educate and train our children—the next generation!

God gave us the mandate to establish his rule and bring order, and he gave us the authority to do so. He gave us the dominion mandate in the garden.

In fact, within Jewish circles, this mandate from Genesis is not called the dominion mandate as we call it within church circles; it's called the cultural mandate. Jewish tradition teaches that we must influence culture because the word God spoke is *radah*, which is primarily translated as "to rule or to have dominion" (Genesis 1:26, 28; Leviticus 25:46). But the second meaning is "to scrape or to scrape out," as in the context of plowing or cultivation. We have the capacity to break up hard ground and cultivate it. In other words, to create, advance, maintain, and bring forth culture. What culture? The culture of the kingdom of God.

Through Christ, we have the authority to influence the world, and through the Holy Spirit, we have the power to transform the world.

Throughout the coming chapters, we are going to help you restory your family and put tools in your hands so you can begin the journey of building your dynastic household—your oikos. And because of your faithfulness to God, as a result of his blessing, your children's children are going to give God the glory for what you began. As we begin, let's look to the Apostle Paul to learn where this truth comes from:

> For this reason I kneel before the Father, from whom every family in heaven and on earth derives its name. I pray that out of his glorious riches he may strengthen you with power through his Spirit in your inner being, so that Christ may dwell in your hearts through faith. And I pray that you, being rooted and established in love, may have power, together with all the Lord's holy people, to grasp how wide and long and high and deep is the love of Christ, and to know this love that surpasses knowledge—that you may be filled to the measure of all the fullness of God. Now to him who is able to do immeasurably more than all we ask or imagine, according to his power that is at work within us, to him be glory in the church and in Christ Jesus throughout all generations, for ever and ever! Amen. (Ephesians 3:14-21)

Did you notice, right at the very beginning, that Paul is praising God? Why? Because God is the one who gives identity to every family. He gives us our names. Yahweh created us in his image and gave us our names. And whom did he name? Every family in heaven and on earth. And found within a name is identity, belonging, mission, and mandate.

Also, intriguing is how Paul uses the word "every" before the word family; in Greek, this means "every type of." He says every type of family—those broken or restored, ones led by single moms or grandparents, those that have prodigal children and those that have no children, the nuclear, generational, and those who may already have the beginnings of a dynastic focus—all families are given their name by God! It is not too much to say that families, and the restoration thereof, are at the heart of the love of God.

In Ephesians 3, Paul is saying that God intends to give hope to every family. He has a purpose. He has a mission and a mandate for every single family on earth. But each mission and mandate collectively come together in the whole family of God. That's why he uses the words *whole* and *every kind*. As you pursue God's will, this includes you and your family, and it also includes all believing families on earth—the whole royal dynasty of God!

Your Family Narrative

This is where your journey begins, at the beginning, with the first step toward a dynastic family. We want to help you re-story your family narrative because doing so unlocks hope and a future. It provides a vision and a sense of mandate and mission. As your family dynasty grows in number and influence, where the generations will have many different gifted family members, each should be encouraged to embrace their gifts and individual assignments but to do so within the context of a family mission.

For some, the idea that God has a purpose for every kind of family—even yours—is difficult to embrace. I know the heartache. I know the struggle. I know the confusion that comes from looking at the rest of the world and observing what seems to be happy families all around you while you merely eke by, struggling to survive in your own family. You wonder how you could ever possibly make a difference in the world. If you are in this category and are maybe even growing frustrated by all this talk about family and generations and dynasty and purpose, I want to encourage you to jump to the epilogue of this book. There you will find a personal letter to the "nonfamily" families. I used the phrase "nonfamily" intentionally as I want to draw your attention to the lie (and one that has probably been said to you) that you and your family dynamic are somehow insufficient. This is simply not true! It is God who makes you, me, and every kind of family, sufficient to receive his love and blessing. So please read my pastoral letter to you and then come back here and confidently take your next step.

When taking the first step forward, it is invaluable to look back at your family heritage. When you do, you will identify the essence of your mission. You'll see a pattern. As you reflect on prior generations, you will identify good and bad. You will see how your life and family fit together in a way that you have never seen before!

It's not about being religious and having a long religious to-do list: Bible study, spending time in prayer, giving to the church. It is about resting in the peace of the lordship of Christ. Peace is the greatest weapon of God in this spiritual and natural warfare on earth, and Jesus is the source of our peace (John 14:27, Philippians 4:7, Romans 5:1, Colossians 3:15). Satan knows that if he undermines peace, creates fear, and divides people, churches, and families, he will continue to exercise dominion and build his mini dynasties.

But I have great news for the church and terrible news for the evil one! The church is building dynastic families in the kingdom of God. And in doing so, it is God's people who will transform communities, regions, and nations to the glory of God.

In the coming pages, you'll discover your family's place in the grand story of God. Together, we'll discover how dynastic families:

- Embrace the dominion mandate as a family
- Identify your God-given family name and mission
- Engage children and grandchildren with a seat at the table
- Grow your capacity to exercise their dominion
- Create an environment in which each member can thrive
- Take the first step toward reconciling prodigals
- Influence your church and communities

Spoiler alert—it all begins with trust, which is the total opposite of everything Satan does. He is a liar whose kingdom is built upon a weak foundation of lies. What's curious is the word *satan* is actually not a name but an attribute. In Hebrew, the word means "adversary, one who plots against another." Satan plots against us. He accuses us of our sins. He seeks to deceive us. He is the father of lies. Every aspect of his work here on earth to build his kingdom is rooted in the very first lie that he spoke in the garden: "Did God really say…?"

As a testimony of God's grace, allow me to share with you the power of God's persistent love and forgiveness as experienced by multiple generations of the Turner family of New Zealand.

The Turner Family

Edward Turner and Maude Constable immigrated from Cambridge, England, in 1885. Edward fled to New Zealand under dishonorable circumstances, abandoning his pregnant wife and their children in favor of a new life with Maude.

After arriving in Auckland, Edward, an experienced grower and retailer of produce and flowers, began his new life in Auckland—New Zealand's largest city. Following the death of their baby daughter, they moved to the country and lived off the land, half a day's horseback ride from the city. The family grew, and they had nine sons following their daughter.

While Edward had left a trail of relational pain behind in England, after the death of his daughter, he must have felt his sins were being punished. Living off the land may have been a way to escape the pain; however, God had not forgotten him. It was during these difficult days that he and Maude met a Brethren lay preacher who, after several visits to the town, began staying with the Turners when in the area. Mr. Rimmer told Edward and Maude about what it means to have personal faith in Jesus, and over time, he led them in their decisions to become Christians. Edward and Maude became committed believers and started taking the family to church where some of the boys even met their future wives.

Meanwhile, Edward's fruit business went from strength to strength and, under the leadership of his sons, expanded. He eventually sold to his sons, and they expanded the retail operation and developed the wholesale business, which in time became known as Turners and Growers. T&G became one of the 100 largest companies in New Zealand.

One of the sons, Harvey, had a keen business acumen and spearheaded the growth of the company. By the early 1970s, there were seventeen family members across three generations working side by side in the company, with most of the nine brothers still working (albeit part-time by then), plus seven members of the third generation and three of the fourth generation. The senior management was in the hands of two of Harvey's sons, Jack and Grahame, both committed Christians, just as Harvey was. Jack and Grahame pioneered the Chinese gooseberry export business. They decided the name wouldn't work well in America and changed the name to *Kiwifruit*, a name that was subsequently adopted worldwide.

Edward and Maude's descendants became influential people in New Zealand and beyond. Their family includes members of Parliament, a knight, mayors, city councilors, pastors, Christian business leaders, leaders in local churches, and missionaries to India, Papua New Guinea, and beyond. Grahame and Jack were decorated war heroes, serving in World War II.

After his retirement, Grahame, who had heard rumors of his grandfather's checkered past, did some research and was devastated and shocked when he learned about the true family history. He and his brother Jack started to reach out to some of their grandfather's descendants. They made connections with some of them and even brought some to New Zealand and had them stay in their homes. Other descendants moved to South Africa. They had become Christians as well. Grahame and Jack invited them to New Zealand where they met and reconciled their family's long history of brokenness and pain.

The Turner family's beautiful reconciliation is a testimony to the redemptive nature of God and the power of having a place of belonging and a seat at the family table. And for many of your families, the journey toward family reconciliation is waiting. It is a scary place to be because the lies of the world are loud. The regrets are strong. The pain runs deep. The Turner family continues to build on this legacy, using it to fuel their dynastic mandate. They are now expanding multiple businesses across numerous industries, all to the glory of God.

But know this, God is at work in the heavens and on earth. And our dynastic families are to be *in* this world but not *of* this world; this is the place God has for us, living in a world that is battling for truth. We can trust in his goodness as we embrace his intent and purpose for families—yours and mine included. We can take the next step in re-storying our families even while surrounded by lies.

Reflection Questions

1. Scripture teaches that all believers are empowered with the Holy Spirit. He is the believer's source of power. How have you experienced his power in your life? Explain using the biblical references provided on page 40-41.
2. Through the dunamis (power) provided by the Holy Spirit, believers have the authority to build dynastic families to advance and expand territory, wealth, rule, and governance in the kingdom of God. Does this inspire you? Encourage you? Or even intimidate you? Explain.
3. Created in God's image, every family in heaven and on earth has been given a name. In that name is our identity, belonging, mission, and mandate. What are yours?
4. The church is the place were God builds and equips dynastic families. How is God's church being used to build up your family? Give examples.

5
DID GOD REALLY SAY...?

It is only by believing in God that we can ever criticize the Government. Once abolish . . . God, and the Government becomes the God. That fact is written all across human history. The truth is that Irreligion is the opium of the people. Where the people do not believe in something beyond the world, they will worship the world. But, above all, they will worship the strongest thing in the world.

~ G.K. Chesterton, *Christendom in Dublin*

Fanciful and dreamy stories have come to grip the imaginations of our collective culture. Perhaps none more powerfully than Cinderella. This folk tale, also known as "The Little Glass Slipper," stretches itself back more than 2,000 years and has untold variations throughout the world. From the Americas to the Korean Peninsula and throughout Europe, Africa, and Asia, readers have been tantalized with the tale of a young girl who was pressed into servitude. The most common version, familiar to American readers, is that of Charles Perrault, written in French and published in 1697.

The beautiful young Cinderella is the daughter of a wealthy gentleman. But her stepmother and stepsisters bemoan her beauty and force Cinderella into behaving like a hired maid, completing all of the household chores. I can imagine the three women harassing Cinderella with lies about who she is, taunting her with lies about her father's love, and mocking her about her pitiful life. Lies, lies, and more lies.

But Cinderella is no maid. Through a series of wonderful and otherworldly events, Cinderella discovers her true worth, marries the prince, and then forgives and redeems her once-nagging sisters—even granting them status and marriage in the house of the prince. It's a beautiful and powerful tale in any language.

What is it about stories that we find so captivating? We find C.S. Lewis' answer to this question in his classic book *Mere Christianity*. "If we find ourselves with a desire that nothing in this world can satisfy, the most probable explanation is that we were made for another world."[1] And while Lewis' assessment is true, it's also notable that we were made by a loving God from another world. Even Perrault acknowledged God as the giver of all that is good, and he champions wielding our gifts for the common good: "Without a doubt, it is a great advantage to have intelligence, courage, good breeding, and common sense. These, and similar talents come only from heaven, and it is good to have them. However, even these may fail to bring you success, without the blessing of a godfather or a godmother."[2]

Indeed, we were made for another world but purposed to live in this one.

The Called-Out Ones

Traditionally, the theology of the church has identified the collective body of believers as those who are called by God. And this is true. But much like Paul's teaching in Ephesians, we need to understand God is the determiner of both the one and the many. Just as God has named every family, he has called out each son and daughter as well as all believers—the *ekklesia*.

Understanding the ekklesia (and its alternate spelling ecclesia) is important in responding to the dominion mandate. This Greek word was used often by the New Testament writers, and it is most commonly translated as "church" in our English Bibles. Examples include when Saul and Barnabas met with Christians in Antioch (Acts 11:26), when Paul confessed to having persecuted the church (1 Corinthians 15:9), and when Peter used *ekklesia* to proclaim Christians have been called out of this world and "into his wonderful light" (1 Peter 2:9). The church is the place where the ekklesia—the called-out ones—gather together.

God is the God of the many and the one. He is the Sovereign Lord over the multitude, the church, and the one—the Christian. God calls each of us, and all of us, to separate ourselves from sin (1 Peter 1:16), to fellowship with other believers (Acts 2:42), and to be a light to the world (Matthew 5:14). This is the responsibility of you and me, of your family and mine, of your church and my church, and every person called by God around the globe. But what does this look like?

> *We are called by God (again, his calling and our mandate). We are born into families. And we are mandated to act according to the purposes he initiated before the fall in the garden. We are to seek to forgive and redeem.*

In Paul's letter to the Romans, believers are instructed "in view of God's mercy, to offer your bodies as a living sacrifice, holy and pleasing to God—this is your true and proper worship. Do not conform to the pattern of this world, but be transformed by the renewing of your mind. Then you will be able to test and approve what God's will is—his good, pleasing and perfect will" (Romans 12:1-2). And what is God's "good, pleasing and perfect will?" It was first revealed to Adam and Eve, was reiterated to Noah and his sons, and was perfectly proclaimed by Jesus. We are to make disciples by fulfilling the first command to love God. We are to make disciples by fulfilling the command that is equal to it: to love our neighbors. And we are to make disciples by fulfilling the mandate to be fruitful, multiplying, filling the earth, and ruling with his will set before us as our only guide—all in response to his blessing.

Here is the rub—we have an enemy who asks us, "Did God really say...?" The father of lies is at work, and his work is devastating people everywhere. Families are falling apart. Churches are teaching anything and everything but the name of Jesus Christ. Idols, crime, and sin fill our communities. What are we to do?

We are to look for the truth in a world of lies. John tells us much about how to live in the truth of Jesus Christ: "Do not love the world or anything in the world. If anyone loves the world, love for the Father is not in them. For everything in the world—the lust of the flesh, the lust of the eyes, and the pride of life—comes not from the Father but from the world. The world and its desires pass away, but whoever does the will of God lives forever" (1 John 2:15-17).

The world is full of lies, and they all begin with, "Did God really say...?" The devil does not decry the words of God directly; he subverts them, confuses them, and misuses them. Perhaps you've never considered it, but the lies of the world—the lust of the flesh, the lust of the eyes, and the pride of life—began in the garden.

Attacking the Dominion Mandate

The dominion mandate in Genesis 1:28 is the foundation for human activity in the world, and it's what is under attack by Satan. A prime example of the ways of the evil one is recorded in the account of Jesus' temptation in the wilderness:

> Jesus, full of the Holy Spirit, left the Jordan and was led by the Spirit into the wilderness, where for forty days he was tempted by the devil. He ate nothing during those days, and at the end of them he was hungry.
>
> The devil said to him, "If you are the Son of God, tell this stone to

become bread." Jesus answered, "It is written: 'Man shall not live on bread alone.'"

The devil led him up to a high place and showed him in an instant all the kingdoms of the world. And he said to him, "I will give you all their authority and splendor; it has been given to me, and I can give it to anyone I want. If you worship me, it will all be yours."

Jesus answered, "It is written: 'Worship the Lord your God and serve him only.'"

The devil led him to Jerusalem and had him stand on the highest point of the temple. "If you are the Son of God," he said, "throw yourself down from here. For it is written:

'He will command his angels concerning you,
    to guard you carefully;
  they will lift you up in their hands,
    so that you will not strike your foot against a stone.'"

Jesus answered, "It is said, '"Do not put the Lord your God to the test.'"

When the devil had finished all this tempting, he left him until an opportune time.

Jesus returned to Galilee in the power of the Spirit, and news about him spread through the whole countryside. He was teaching in their synagogues, and everyone praised him.
    (Luke 4:1-15)

These three temptations by Satan in the wilderness are but three of the many temptations Jesus faced while on earth. And they are the three most common to people. They are the lust of the flesh (vs. 2-4), the pride of life (vs. 5-8), and the lust of the eyes (vs. 9-12). What will we do when our bodies ache with hunger pains and the many woes of suffering? What will we do when we are enticed by the promises of success and wealth in the world? What will we do when others want to prop us up as worldly gods, kings, princes, and princesses? The answer to this is in God's covenant with Adam and Eve, and by extension, you and me: we are to follow his call and fulfill our mandate.

We have to understand the devil is at work trying to maintain and expand his control of the kingdoms of the world (Ephesians 2:2). He knows he does not have any influence over the kingdom of God, or the church (Matthew 16:1-20), for Jesus built the church on the truth of his identity as the Son of the Living God, having overcome every temptation and lived a sinless life (2 Corinthians 5:21; 1 John 3:5), and suffered the wages of sin on our behalf, (Hebrews 7:27), and who is now raised from the dead (Acts 2:24), and sits at the right hand of God wielding the power and authority of heaven on earth (1 Peter 3:22). And nothing can overcome it!

Yet the devil is at work doing what he always does—lying to God's children and promising them every good thing under the sun so long as they turn away from him. And many of us do so because we believe the lie.

Authors Chuck Colson and Nancy Pearcy answer the question throughout their landmark book *How Now Shall We Live?* They suggest that God has already given us our answer. The truth is that we have known from the beginning how to live—it is the dominion mandate. But Colson and Pearcy do an excellent job of explaining what this looks like in our day-to-day lives. Their book explains:

> Christianity is more than a personal relationship with Jesus Christ. It is also a worldview that not only answers life's basic questions—Where did we come from, and who are we? What has gone wrong with the world? What can we do to fix it?—but also shows us how we should live as a result of those answers. *How Now Shall We Live?* gives Christians the understanding, the confidence, and the tools to confront the world's bankrupt worldviews and to restore and redeem every aspect of contemporary culture: family, education, ethics, work, law, politics, science, art, music. This [truth] will change

every Christian who reads it. It will change the church in the new millennium.[3]

We couldn't agree more!

Ever since humanity was exiled from the Garden of Eden, having lost the kingdom, we have been empire-building. And this empire-building—which is always individualistic at best and narcissistic at worst—is rooted in the lust of the flesh, the lust of the eyes, and the pride of life. As such, it has devastating effects on the world!

But families are standing in the gap, faithfully wielding the authority of Christ through the blessing they have been given: they are dynastic families—whether by design or spiritual intuition—that understand their capacity to govern and rule as God intends is dependent upon their generational wealth.

The DeVos Family

Many in America know the name Betsy DeVos, while few know the names of the DeVos and Prince (Betsy's maiden name) families, but we should. Betsy DeVos, a longtime advocate for education, was thrust onto the national scene when President Donald Trump selected her to be the eleventh United States Secretary of Education, a position she held from 2017 to 2021.

The DeVos family, upon simple examination, can be seen as an exemplar of Christian engagement in what is often referred to as the "Seven Mountains" or "Seven Spheres," which originated with Loren Cunningham and Bill Bright, founders of Youth With a Mission (YWAM) and Campus Crusade for Christ (CRU), respectively. These seven areas of society are the realms in which Christians must engage to effectively establish dominion (bring forth godly governance) and help every man, woman, and child flourish in the blessing of the Lord. They are arts and entertainment, business, education, family, government, media, and religion.

They say the apple doesn't fall far from the tree; well, Betsy comes from a good tree firmly rooted in great soil. Her parents are Edgar and Elsa Prince. Elsa is one of the greatest patrons of literature, art, and culture in Michigan and across the United States. And Edgar became one of the wealthiest men in Michigan through his business acumen, which helped him and his business partners succeed in the manufacturing industry while employing thousands of people. However, unsatisfied with limiting his efforts to only one sphere of influence, Prince supported the founding of the Family Research Council under the leadership of Dr. James Dobson. And through their affiliation with the Acton Institute, a "think-tank whose mission is to promote a free and virtuous society characterized by individual liberty and sustained by religious principles," Betsy and her husband, Dick, have led the family's efforts to invest more than $1.2 billion into Christian work, shaping the education and business systems in various regions of the world and reducing poverty at every turn.

Continuing in the family tradition of helping artists and enhancing communities, their son Rick DeVos founded the Grand Rapids ArtPrize festival, which is supported in part by the family's various foundations. "Since its inception in 2009, millions have participated in ArtPrize, displaying their work, opening their spaces to artists and visitors from around the world, and sparking countless conversations about what art is and why it matters."[4]

Humans have a nearly visceral longing of the heart to know what art is and why it matters. Yet there is a more important question that lies deep within every human soul as to why it matters. People around the world need Christians to be a part of the conversation about what art is and why it matters because we are the only ones who have the answer and because God calls us to share it!

We have the Spirit of God who increases our knowledge of truth through the saving grace of Jesus. And it is in this truth that we share in the life and work of Jesus "to seek and to save the lost" (Luke 19:10), act in humility and obedience (Philippians 2:5-8), extend compassion (Matthew 9:36), and depend on God in prayer (Luke 5:16). It is this dependence on God and adherence to his will and commands that leads His called-out ones to make a difference in the world. By embracing his calling, we can exercise dominion for the sake of his kingdom and the benefit of people everywhere.

Let us now turn our attention to the components of the dominion mandate and discover how Satan—in his effort to gain control of more and more kingdoms of this world—turns each one upside down in our fallen world. We will juxtapose God's truth with the pale version of it offered by the deceiver so we, as the ekklesia (the called-out ones), can know how to live in this world while we "set [our] minds on things above, not earthly things" (Colossians 3:2).

God Blessed Them

God says we—all men and all women—are made in his image. And through the presence of the Father, the lordship of the Son, and the power of the Holy Spirit who dwells in us, we have the capacity—the dunamis—to love and create as he does.

Satan says something very different. *You are your own mirror and have the power to create your own good nature. You are the pinnacle achievement of human evolution. There is no one like you. Go and help other people be like you. You rightfully deserve the seat of honor. You can become the blessing the world needs: you just need to be more like yourself.*

God gave the Mandate to Adam and Eve

God says we are to act according to his will; we should, as husband and wife, and by extension, our families, abide by his will on earth as it is in heaven. And while cultures and traditions may have relegated women to a lesser status, from the very beginning, God made men and women equal and perfectly fit for one another.

Satan deceives many by doubting the historical realities of Adam and Eve. He says, there was no person named Adam, nor was there an Eve. *You don't really believe in a literal Adam, do you? That is just a fairytale made up by people who don't believe in science and just want to justify their immoral view about women. Are you really listening to that man in the pulpit? He's just a bully, always demeaning women, demanding they submit. Women are too evolved to believe something so silly as supporting a man in a committed relationship.*

We are to Be Fruitful in all our Endeavors

God says his creative work is the most important work, and our work to create and govern carries similar importance so long as it aligns with his work. We are to live, love, and create in an effort to bring glory to God and his redeeming power to people, no matter what work we do and where we choose to do it.

Satan says to follow your dreams. *There is only one you. You are unique. You can be anything you want to be. Are your talents not your own? Shouldn't you use them to advance your own career first so you can later help other people if you want to? It is prudent to be secure and save for the future. You don't want to be foolish with your money, giving it away to other people, do you? What will happen when you don't have anymore? You don't want to be a burden to them, do you? Take what you have, be comfortable, drink wine, and be merry.*

We are to Multiply, Creating Biological and Spiritual Disciples

God says there is no higher calling than to fill the whole world with the glory of his name. And we are to do this by training our children in the commandments of God and teaching others to follow Jesus and become his disciples. We invite people to engage in the transcendent purpose of God's kingdom by bringing understanding and a deep sense of belonging both in the natural (dynasty) and spiritual (body of Christ) families. And together, we live out the grand story of God!

Satan says it is selfish to have children. *Do you not see the suffering in the world? Why would you want to bring a person into the world? They are only going to suffer and die. And don't you know the world's resources are limited? We can't afford to feed another mouth. And what about the impact on the climate? Don't you care about the environment that you believe God created?*

We are to Bring Order and Hope to the World

God says we have the privilege and purpose to join him in his grand plan of reconciling people to himself; we are to steward creation, prune gardens, create businesses, protect the orphan and the widow, hold those who do evil accountable for their actions, and show the watching world there is a better way, or more righteous way to live. We, the dynastic families of God, manifest the glory of his kingdom, provoking the world to jealousy of the love and kingship of God.

Satan says we should pay no attention to the world, for we were made for another world. *Yes, this world is beautiful, and I'll give it to you if you want it, and you really do. After all, this is the only world you have. You only have one life to live, so you might as well make the best of it. And since you have only your life, you should find meaning inside yourself. That is the only hope you have to make sense of the world. Just take care of your family. You don't need to meddle in other people's families. You don't really think your family is better than theirs, do you? Keep to yourself. Keep your family safe. Let other people do the same. We are all in this together, but each of us is on our own journey, aren't we? Besides, everyone has everything they need; the government is making sure people have food, education, and medical care. Isn't it wonderful that people are committed to educating other people's children? How noble!*

The Reformation

More than 500 years ago, there was a movement that started in Europe, which blossomed into what many refer to as the Protestant Church. This movement became known as the Reformation: it was the greatest religious and political upheaval in western civilization since the fall of the Roman Empire. Its leaders are often referred to by their last names: Martin Luther, Ulrich Zwingli, and John Calvin. It stemmed from a desire to reform the Catholic Church of Rome by separating truth from lie and ushering in an age of reform, bringing the church back to its humble roots of proclaiming "Jesus and Jesus alone" and focusing on the Word of God and not the teachings of man.

This movement transformed Europe and ultimately the world. Most surprising may be that this movement took hold not solely in the cathedrals, castles, or colleges, but in the homes of thousands of peasant farmers. Out of the Reformation came the Farmhouse Movement. Far too much reflection on the Farmhouse Movement focuses on the idea that these were merely peasants to whom the Bible was now available. This narrow focus fails to understand these were farmers on family land, and they began to understand and educate themselves and their children in the Scriptures. These families grew in strength, number, and influence because of their focus on God and their families. Fascinatingly, the German word for house (haus) means household!

This movement produced incredibly creative ideas for many areas of industrial plowing and industry that increased their yield. The families became wealthier and more influential while carrying the kingdom and having a heart for transformation. It was this movement that seeded the success of the American story birthed by family-minded, spiritual patriarchs and matriarchs who would one day settle the American colonies. Their Atlantic crossing was not only a quest for religious freedom but a pursuit of a new place of dominion, to the glory of God.

Belonging to Christ

In essence, dynastic families deep-rooted in the legacy of farmhouses are the foundation of this nation and its prosperity, regardless of race, color, or creed. Christians and their families, who are saved by God's grace, have a special place in this world. We have been called to be a part of what God is doing.

First, we belong to Jesus, and we can stand confidently before God because "there is now no condemnation for those who are in Christ Jesus" (Romans 8:1). We are part of the bride of Christ, and we should celebrate that our names are written in the Book of Life for all eternity (John 10:28-30; Philippians 4:3; Revelation 3:5).

Second, we are part of a family with a God-given name and identity, as well as a purpose to join him as helpmates (Genesis 2:18). God uses the redeemed lives of broken men and women to heal the lives of broken men and women. In Christ, our families get to be a part of God's work to restore and reconcile the world to himself.

And we don't have to go it alone. Jesus promises to be with us: "Then Jesus came to them and said, 'All authority in heaven and on earth has been given to me. Therefore go and make disciples of all nations, baptizing them in the name of the Father and of the Son and of the Holy Spirit, and teaching them to obey everything I have commanded you. And surely I am with you always, to the very end of the age'" (Matthew 28:18-20).

As part of the body of Christ (the church), there is no distinction among us, for God does not play favorites: "Just as a body, though one, has many parts, but all its many parts form one body, so it is with Christ. For we were all baptized by one Spirit to form one body —whether Jews or Gentiles, slave or free—and we were all given the one Spirit to drink. Even so, the body is not made up of one part but of many" (1 Corinthians 12:12-14). These many parts of the body have different gifts from that same Spirit.

We belong to Christ. We belong in family. And our family belongs in a church.

But what happens if we Christians relegate ourselves to personal piety and leave the world to fend for itself? Well, for those of us who are guided by the work of the Holy Spirit, and have the mind of Christ, and thus know the will of the Father, we understand the world is not supposed to look the way it does. We see it plainly that if we do not stand in the gap between heaven and hell, taking our place in the spiritual battle, the world, and its people will be consumed by the lies of the deceiver and go about building their own empires against the will of God.

It has been said by our Founding Fathers that if you want to create a good society, even if it is not a religious one, the best society is one in which the Judeo-Christian worldview is taught and followed. Our American founders believed this to be true. John Adams, a signer of the Declaration of Independence and the second president of the United States, said of our society and our governing purpose, "Our Constitution was made only for a moral and religious people. It is wholly inadequate to the government of any other."[5]

God has given us his love so we can give it away! God has given us faith so we can share it with others. And God provides for our needs so we can provide for others.

In the early 1990s, David Barton of Wall Builders led an exhaustive research study to quantify the social effects of eliminating prayer from school. Gathering data from government and educational reports between 1951 and 1993, their research concluded there was a cultural and moral demise since the elimination of prayer from public schools:

- Violent crimes were up from 150,000 offenses in 1951 to 1,900,000 in 1993, far outpacing population growth.
- Sexually transmitted diseases in ten to fourteen-year-olds were up from a low of 14 cases per 100,000 in 1962 to a high of 70 cases in 1990.

- Average SAT scores plummeted from a high of 980 in 1962 to a low of 890 in 1980.
- The birthrate for unwed girls fifteen to nineteen years old jumped from 1.5 % of all births in 1962 to 4.5 % in 1993.
- The number of single-parent households increased from about 4.8 million in 1962 to just over 12 million in 1993, again at a rate that exceeded the population growth.[6]

I wonder how shocked we would be if we were to again examine the social and cultural shift, this time focusing on the change during the last thirty years. What would we find if we dared to conduct the same research? My guess is it would be more of the same because Christian families are not embracing God's mandate to rule over the world. Perhaps it's because we believe the lies, and we are distracted by the pale glory of another.

John Calvin, the French theologian, pastor, and reformer, famously said, "The human heart is a perpetual idol factory." God knows it. You and I know it. Satan knows it.

When we remove God from our daily lives, we will create our own idols to worship, whether it be Marxism, Critical Race Theory, climate change, abortion, big government, big business, the US Constitution, political activism, hobbies, work, church, or ourselves. No matter what we focus on, if it is anything other than God, it is in vain.

But when we focus on God, wielding our authority as dynastic families, and doing so with each member using their gifting for the edification of the body of Christ and to the benefit of the world, we can, by the power of the Holy Spirit, in the name of Jesus, to the glory of the Father, re-story the lives of the people around us.

Reflection Questions

1. The church is the place where the ekklesia—God's called-out ones—gather together. Why is this important?

2. The dominion mandate in Genesis 1:28 was given to God's people. But it was also attacked by Satan. Why do you think he questioned it? Explain.
3. What are the primary differences between building the kingdom of God and empire building? Why are these distinctions important?
4. Satan attacks the dominion mandate in many ways (highlighted on pages 57-59). Which way do you see as the most destructive? Why?
5. We belong to Christ, we belong in family, and our family belongs in church. How have you seen/experienced the importance of these three elements in your own life? Explain.

6
FAMILY DYNASTY EXERCISED IS DOMINION ENACTED

This is what the L*ord* *Almighty, the God of Israel, says to all those
I carried into exile from Jerusalem to Babylon: "Build houses
and settle down; plant gardens and eat what they produce. Marry and have
sons and daughters; find wives for your sons and give your daughters in
marriage, so that they too may have sons and daughters. Increase in number
there; do not decrease. Also, seek the peace and prosperity of the city
to which I have carried you into exile. Pray to the* L*ord* *for it,
because if it prospers, you too will prosper."*

~ Jeremiah 29:4-7

The story of the transformation of Huntington, West Virginia, is a story of Jesus' rule in the kingdom of God, the love that God has for his people, and the power of the Holy Spirit to empower and purpose Christians. This is what happens when family dynasty results in Christian dominion. And it is good! We see this plainly in the transformation of the lives of the people of Huntington.

As you read this story of the families involved in Huntington's dramatic turnaround, revel in the glory of God manifesting through our brothers and sisters in Christ. Embrace the idea of your family being more geographically connected and closer to each other emotionally and spiritually. Listen to the conversations between grandparents and grandchildren discussing how to care for the poor in your community. And begin to envision how your city would look if your family aligned strategically with other families in investing the love of God into your community. Would boarded-up buildings be replaced by family-owned businesses? Would empty lots grow into community gardens? Would fewer people be sleeping at the homeless shelter? More moms and dads attending PTA meetings and serving on school boards? Less drug use? No more sex trafficking? Fewer murders? No more suicides?

God's capacity to redeem humanity through the faithfulness of dynastic families is boundless! There is hope and renewal to be had in every community around the world. Trudie and I are humbled by the invitation to be part of what God is doing in a small city on the Ohio River.

It was 2011, and a lawyer was listening to the Lord. Aware of the plight of the people of Huntington, he was seeking a way to help. Believing God had a plan, a purpose, and a message for his good friend and pastor Mike Greider, he suggested Mike attend a leadership conference in Dallas and paid for his expenses. And it was there, while speaking at the conference, that I met Mike and learned about the grief of the people of Huntington.

I was one of the keynote speakers and addressed the attendees on the topics of city and community transformation as well as family dynasty being the key to dominion, which is the catalyst for city-wide restoration. Mike was in the room for both sessions; after the second session, he approached me with a burning desire to learn more. We met for a few minutes afterward, and his story grabbed my attention and gripped my heart. He expressed that he and others in his community had been praying for their hometown for almost twenty years, asking God to heal the hearts and lives of the people. And through that prayer, God was opening doors. They had meaningful relationships with city leaders: they all knew something could be done that would change the city, but they did not yet know what that would be until he heard the heart of God expressed in the dominion mandate revealed in the Scriptures.

Mike asked me to visit with him, his friend Audy Perry, and Huntington's newly elected Mayor, Steve Williams, back in Huntington. I agreed. And together with my dear friend and economist Elijah Low, who has been instrumental in developing much of our dominion strategy, we prayed, planned, and, ultimately, challenged local families to embrace their dominion authority for the betterment of the people of the Huntington community. They received our challenge with a posture of humility, a heart to serve, and an intentionality to engage. These families were willing!

What happened next can only be explained in terms of the miraculous. The transformation that occurred in the coming years because of the faithfulness of God and the humble workings of the city's civic, church, and business leaders—as well as many local families—made national headlines. The transformation captured the attention of the world because it was on the heels of two Netflix documentaries: *Heroin(e)*[1] and *Recovery Boys*[2] (made only six months prior), which highlighted the agony of the community.

Huntington, West Virginia, and its neighbor across the border, Ashland, Kentucky, had the heartbreaking distinction of being rated the worst community for overall well-being in a 2013 Gallup Poll. But what might be even worse is the acknowledgment that this season of hardship was not an isolated incident, as the same survey in previous years found that "Huntington-Ashland also trailed all other metros in 2008, 2010, and 2011."[3]

When I arrived in Huntington to meet with this trio of local leaders, I did not find a despondent soul in the room. They knew the plight of the community and were confident the cities could be restored. But how bad was the pain of the people?

The Huntington metro area was the worst rated in the nation by a number of measures. Respondents were the most likely Americans to report physical health problems, with exceptionally high rates of diabetes, cancer diagnoses, and chronic pain. More than 34.4% reported high cholesterol, and 46.9% reported high blood pressure last year, both the most of any metro area and perhaps leading to the high rate of heart attacks reported. Nearly one in ten people surveyed stated they had previously suffered a heart attack, more than in any other area. Nearly 40% reported they were obese last year, the highest rate in the nation. Similarly, no metro area scored worse for emotional health than Huntington, where residents were more likely to say they felt worried or depressed than anywhere else in America. Residents also had lower overall evaluations of their current lives and future prospects than respondents in any other metro area.[4]

But God.

Our visit started with a brief meeting with Mike, Audy, and Mayor Williams, and it quickly morphed into a series of gatherings over the next few days where we discussed the brutal facts, and Elijah and I shared God's plan and dream for cities (see Isaiah 65).

Leveraging their social equity, Audy and his father Mike invited other notable and influential families from the community to join our discussions and vision casting. Soon, the meetings grew, and the Manns and Lawrence families (and many others) were joined by the president of Marshal University and the CEO of Cabell Huntington Hospital. We were all leaning forward in our chairs, excited about the future of the city.

The Manns Family

It is hard to be excited by the future when you are strapped with debt from the past. And so it was with Huntington as the city was on the verge of facing a legal judgment of $20 million or more had it not settled. The other named party? Huntington Marine Services, which is owned by the Manns family.

Michael Manns is the CEO of the family business and owns the company with his brothers Stephen and Matthew. Started by their parents, Dale and Carolyn, in December 1977, Superior Marine Ways, Inc. is a significant barge and port management company serving the tri-state region of Ohio, Kentucky, and West Virginia. (Perhaps it is my bias, but my favorite part of the family business is that there are multiple generations of family members working in business today!)

Following a two-decade legal battle with the city, the Manns family had a powerful vision for their family dynasty. They took ownership of the future of the city and walked away from a sure thing in court by settling their lawsuit against the city that would have awarded their company more than $20 million in damages. Not only did the Manns family release the city of their legal liability, but they also partnered with the city in the $100 million Harris Riverfront Park project.

Mayor Williams, in his announcement of the project, said of the Manns family, "It says an awful lot about (company ownership) that after twenty years, they went through Hades with the city and this lawsuit . . . Frankly, to put that ill will aside and say we're going to partner with the city of Huntington says a lot about them."[5]

The Perry Family

Audy is a lawyer—and a good one. As he learned more about God's purpose for families, he decided to leave his legal practice and join the family business at Heritage Farms.[6] This act of intentionality is not unfamiliar to the Perry family as "in 1973, co-founders Mike and Henriella Perry decided to relocate from, in Mike's words, 'a beautiful brick home in Huntington, West Virginia, to a burnt log cabin on a 150-acre farm.'"[7] Their love for their Appalachian ancestors drove them into the woods where they would invest nearly twenty years clearing the land, collecting authentic period materials and structures, and building what is now the Heritage Farm Museum

& Village whose mission is "to be a source of hope and renewal for the Appalachian region."[8] Presently, three generations of the family are leading the day-to-day operations of the business.

Understanding the heritage of the region and its people, the Perry family was an integral part of the undergirding of the transformation of the city, both financially and strategically. It was Audy's legal expertise that helped Huntington position Pullman Square[9] as the centerpiece for the downtown revitalization project. Just across the street from Harris Riverfront Park, Pullman Square is the city's new hub of shopping, fine dining, and entertainment.

The Lawrence Family

The Lawrence family of Charleston, West Virginia, was a vital part of advancing the Gospel and seeking community restoration in the Appalachian region more than one hundred years ago. But, following internal family strife that resulted in the murder of the patriarch of the family, the Lawrence family dispersed throughout the globe. By the grace of God, Chuck Lawrence found his way back home, moving to Huntington in 1977.

Originally a businessman in the music-entertainment world, in 1996, Chuck left the business he founded to become the Senior Pastor of Christ Temple Church in Huntington. Chuck and his wife, Jamie, were largely unaware of their family's Gospel-centered framework more than one hundred years ago. During our discussions about the health and financial crisis of the people of the region, many of whom were part of his congregation, I challenged Chuck to learn more about his family history so he could better understand his place in his family dynasty and his role in shaping dynastic households as a pastor.

Today, his brothers and sisters have all moved back to Huntington. They are all part of the church and the community. Each one of them is serving the Lord and loving their neighbors by doing what they are gifted by God to do. Some are in the medical profession, and others own businesses. And once again, many of the children are involved in their family businesses.

The Lawrence family are stewards of the message of family dynasty and dominion both from the pulpit and in various seats of influence in the city. They have been a central part of our modern-day testing of the biblical mandate and the exercise of dominion and governance through family dynasty that leads to the blessing of the earth. What is remarkable, and perhaps even rare within the American church, is that the Lawrences have leveraged the strategy of family dynasty to such a degree that many of the pastors of Christ Temple Church are self-funded through their own family entities, making the church more capable of investing financially in the community. The church is debt-free, and nearly eighty percent of the church's budget is directed toward community engagement and transformation! (This is unheard of in pastoral ministry.)

Their early adoption of the power of dominion through family dynasty has placed Huntington as the de facto public birthplace of the ministry Family Dynasty. Their prayer and reliance on the power of the Holy Spirit is the spiritual undergirding of the transformation of the community. Together, these families played a historic role and continue to lead a remarkable transformation that reveals the power of multiple *oikoses* (households) collaborating and becoming an *oikodomé* (a simultaneously natural and spiritual interworking of families, ostensibly being the local church).

And the world is taking notice of the work in Huntington. In February 2022, Mayor Steve Williams hosted the official launch of the Appalachian Climate Technologies Coalition, "A new coalition anchored by the state's largest cities and universities . . . to make West Virginia's energy industry greener."[10] The Netflix documentaries have been watched in over 190 countries.[11] A dissertation on *Small Town Urban Revitalization: The Effect of Pullman Square on Downtown Huntington, West Virginia* was presented to the Graduate College of Marshall University.[12] NPR identified Huntington as one of the top places for college graduates to live.[13]

Huntington, West Virginia, can easily be understood to be a kingdom within God's kingdom. Author Stephen Dempster explains, "the earth is created for human dominion and rule, which reflects the divine rule. For human beings to function as the image of God, they need a territory, a domain to rule over. And to have the land without human beings is also pointless, for the kingdom needs a king, the dominion a dynasty."[14] These men and women of Huntington, West Virginia, are the princes and princesses ruling under the authority of Christ. Enabled by the purpose of family dynasty, the ministry of the church, and the gifts of the Holy Spirit, these image-bearers of God are living out God's vision for his people.

I am grateful for the ongoing intergenerational work of these families.[15] If it were just the matriarchs and patriarchs of these families who endeavored to serve the people, their efforts would likely fade. But because the children are already engaged in the transformative work in the region, the future is bright!

The Church is the Center of the Community

Tim Keller, founder and former pastor of Redeemer Presbyterian Church in New York City, understood ministry in cities with great clarity. He consistently challenged his congregation, as well as Christians everywhere:

> We should sacrificially lay our lives out for the people in this city. People should see that we care about them, that we love them. Most of all we should offer the righteousness of Jesus Christ to cover their sin, that they may be saved, because he is the priest that those cities need. We, believing in him, can be the priests that our cities need. Look at the cities of the world, look at the masses. God is saying 'why aren't you moved by them?' 'Why aren't you going there?' So let's go.[16]

For too long, an individualistic mindset in the church (and of those Christians who try to "do church" without the actual bride of Christ) has flowed into our communities. This has created a consumer culture that is bending our hearts and minds toward narcissism. For too long, our families and churches have been naval gazing—selfishly abdicating our authority and dominion. For too long, Satan, the deceiver, has been destroying families, churches, and communities because of our selfishness. No longer!

As you embrace the reality that God has a purpose for your family (a universal mandate and a specific mission), I implore you to discover your purpose more fully while connected to the local church. There is strength in numbers. There is confidence in community. There is power in fellowship. God's presence moves in and through God's church.

Remember, your family is crucial to the kingdom of God because families have always been the primary place of belonging in this world. That is not to say families are the only place we belong—we belong *to* our Lord and Savior Jesus Christ, but we also belong *in* family.

If you are not already rooted in a community of worship and accountability, please be a part of a local church: you need them, and they need you. If you and your family are already investing in a local church and living out one of the passages found in the New Testament Scriptures, praise God! Your children, grandchildren, and the generations that follow need to grow up alongside other Christ-centered families in a spiritual community.

Talk with God about his dream for the world. Talk with him about your identity as sons and daughters, princes and princesses.

Make plans to talk with your family about where you believe God wants you all to be going together. Write down the names of other families in your church that you can work with to fill the earth with the glory of God. I'm so excited about what God is doing in your life as you seek him by growing your understanding of his purpose for you and your family. This is such an exciting time for you!

> *Wonder before our holy God about the fairytale you are meant to be living in and run to it.*

It is time to re-story our lives and move beyond the framework of the self-serving unholy trinity of me, myself, and I, and embrace the

God-given framework of family so we can wield the dominion God has purposed for us. And, by the grace of God, we will see how the hope of Christ changes the world because God said,

> *For to us a child is born,*
>   *to us a son is given,*
>   *and the government will be on his shoulders.*
>   *And he will be called*
>   *Wonderful Counselor, Mighty God,*
>   *Everlasting Father, Prince of Peace.*
>   *Of the greatness of his government and peace*
>   *there will be no end.*
>   *He will reign on David's throne*
>   *and over his kingdom,*
>   *establishing and upholding it*
>   *with justice and righteousness*
>   *from that time on and forever.*
> (Isaiah 9:6-7)

I promise you, there are few things in this world as satisfying as building your family dynasty on the life and ministry of Jesus. You are meant to live out your grand family purpose because you have been blessed with the amazing God-given capacity and the presence of God. So, start building your dynasty. The world is waiting!

Reflection Questions

1. What do you see as the primary turning point in the powerful story of Huntington, West Virginia's turnaround? Explain.
2. If you were able to replicate one aspect of this powerful story in your community, what would it be? Why? Take a few moments to journal your answer.

3. Do you believe God's presence moves in and through God's church? Why or why not? How does this influence your personal faith journey and that of your family?
4. We encouraged you to "wonder before our holy God about the fairytale you are meant to be living in and run to it!" How might this exhortation change the way you live?

7
BIBLICAL FAMILIES

There is one body and one Spirit, just as you were called to one hope when you were called; one Lord, one faith, one baptism; one God and Father of all, who is over all and through all and in all. But to each one of us grace has been given as Christ apportioned it. This is why it says: "When he ascended on high, he took many captives and gave gifts to his people.'"

~ Ephesians 4:4-8

Paul helped the early church understand the significance of Christ in our relationship with the Father by using a Greek concept to explain the strength of our relationship. In his letter to the congregation in Ephesus, he wrote, "Praise be to the God and Father of our Lord Jesus Christ, who has blessed us in the heavenly realms with every spiritual blessing in Christ. For he chose us in him before the creation of the world to be holy and blameless in his sight. In love he predestined us for *adoption to sonship* through Jesus Christ, in accordance with his pleasure and will" (Ephesians 1:3-5, emphasis added). This idea of "adoption to sonship" is a legal term referring to the full legal standing of an adopted male heir in Roman culture."[1] Churches plant churches. Disciples make disciples. And parents train up their children who are purposed to be heirs.

Unfortunately, the last 150 years of Christianity have largely been framed by the idea that adoption occurs in the church and is offered at the expense of families. Before a radical transformation of teaching in the mid-1800s, the whole movement of God was tied to families, households, oikoses, especially from the birth of the Protestant Reformation.

The Greek word oikos is exciting. One of the popular passages in which oikos is used is Jesus' teaching in the Sermon on the Mount in Luke 6. The passage is about following Jesus and obeying his teachings. Speaking of the two ways people can respond to his teachings, Jesus says there is the way of the wise and the way of the fool:

> "Why do you call me, 'Lord, Lord,' and do not do what I say? As for everyone who comes to me and hears my words and puts them into practice, I will show you what they are like. They are like a man building a house, who dug down deep and laid the foundation on rock. When a flood came, the torrent struck that house but could not shake it, because it was well built. But the one who hears my words and does not put them into practice is like a man who built a house on the ground without a foundation. The moment the torrent struck that house, it collapsed and its destruction was complete" (6:46-49).

For most of my Christian life, I understood this portion of Scripture to focus on the one man: "He who builds his house on the rock will not be shaken." His work. His house. His calling. His destiny. His life. So long as your life is built on Jesus and nothing else, you will not be shaken. But that's not the emphasis of oikos—the word for "house" in this passage.

The teaching is clear: when the flood rose, the stream broke against the house and could not shake it. The house, built on the teachings of Jesus, could not be overcome by the power of the flood because it was well-built. The house and its inhabitants were built on the truth of Jesus. Throughout the history of mankind, especially before the teachings of Jesus, houses have always been built for a family.

Now, if house means family or household (which would include those who live in my house along with my biological family and me), which it does, would you agree that during the last one hundred years the enemy has been attacking houses?Ced Dads are being ridiculed and disregarded. Moms are being told their value is in their work and not their children.

We are being indoctrinated in worldly thinking that is antagonistic to God while we are told to follow our dreams, embrace our individual calling, and become who we want to be. Why?

Dynasty is Different

Family dynasty is the key to dominion. And dominion is the means of the kingdom breaking through and transforming creation and reconciling people to the Father through Christ. The enemy knows if he can attack families, he can stop (or at least delay) a dimension of the fulfillment of the kingdom: "But the one who hears my words and does not put them into practice is like a man who built a house on the ground without a foundation. The moment the torrent struck that house, it collapsed and its destruction was complete" (Luke 6:49).

As we look at the world, we often see prominent families, celebrities, and politicians crashing down overnight. We marvel at the speed of the fall. But we shouldn't because it's the evidence of how the house has been built, how the family has been built, how the oikos has been built. A house (oikos) built on anything other than Jesus will always collapse, and its destruction will be whole.

During the COVID-19 pandemic, I saw an empire collapse. A prominent real-estate family in California built and was positioned to sell a home for $500 million—meant to be the latest, greatest, largest single-family home ever built. It was designed to have twenty-one bedrooms, forty-one bathrooms, and five pools. Well, the family went bankrupt, and nearly everyone was shocked. But I wasn't shocked at all. During the pandemic, their business practice became unsustainable: the family business could not buy anything, sell anything, or move anything.[2] (As of early 2022, the house was on the market with an asking price of $295 million.)

We can learn from this loss and feel bad for the family, yet the question that must be asked is: how was that oikos built? There are two elements to oikos: family and spiritual. There is a family household, and there is a spiritual household. Both should complement one another, not compete or replace each other.

Within the Christian community, it is common to hear subversive individualistic thinking: It's just me and my family. Our small group is the church. We serve the Lord by connecting with an online church. I don't need the church; I have Jesus. I feel closer to God worshipping on top of a mountain than inside a building. These people are confident in their relationship with God, but they sacrifice fellowship with the bride of Christ. Author Rick McKinley writes of what's missing with this approach in his book *A Kingdom Called Desire:* "Jesus created the community of the church to be a family that comes into being by a new birth in Jesus and the miracle of our union with him. Jesus didn't create a product for us to evaluate and decide if we like it or not."[3]

Today, we also have churches where the thinking is the same even if it looks different: We need more people showing up for prayer night. I can't believe no one thanked me for my sermon. Look at how amazing our youth group leader is. We need to create a podcast! These things are often emphasized based on performance-driven, event-oriented, attraction-modeled churches. And these are the churches where families often get sacrificed on the altar of success.

As we have seen before, the Christian life is comprised of one *and* the whole—both biological and spiritual families. And they cannot be separated because they are both an integral part of God's grand story.

And what is this grand story? It is the story of three great themes of Scripture: the existence of the kingdom of God, the love of God, and God's creation and the purposing of families. One of the best ways to understand this grand story is to view it through the lens of the Old Testament figure Jacob.

Throughout the Bible, the Lord God is referred to as the God of Abraham, Isaac, and Jacob (Genesis 50:24; Exodus 3:15; Acts 7:32). To understand this designation of God's association with these three patriarchs, we must understand God's covenant with Abraham as recorded in Genesis 12:1-3.

> The LORD had said to Abram, "Go from your country, your people and your father's household to the land I will show you.
> "I will make you into a great nation,
>   and I will bless you;
> I will make your name great,
>   and you will be a blessing.
> I will bless those who bless you,
>   and whoever curses you I will curse;
> and all peoples on earth
>   will be blessed through you."

In this conversation with Abraham, God made a promise to all the people of the world. Yes, Abraham (originally Abram) would become the father of a large nation of people. Yes, the name of Abraham would be held in high esteem throughout the world and for all time. Yes, God was unequivocally stating he would be Abraham's provider and protector. But most significant is that God is expressing his intent to bless the people of the earth. That sounds a lot like the dominion/cultural mandate and the Great Commission, does it not?

And God reiterated this blessing to Abraham, mentioning his son Isaac by name. (Genesis 21:12). Then he also expresses to Abraham's grandson, Jacob (Genesis 28:14-15). Moreover, God blessed and renamed Jacob: "God said to him, 'Your name is Jacob, but you will no longer be called Jacob; your name will be Israel.' So he named him Israel. And God said to him, 'I am God Almighty; be fruitful and increase in number. A nation and a community of nations will come from you, and kings will be among your descendants'" (Genesis

35:10-11). God's covenant with the people of the earth is directly related to the original dynastic family of Abraham.

And I find it interesting that God made his covenant with one generation (Abraham), but he reaffirmed it with three, with the third being the father of twelve sons who would become the twelve tribes or households of Israel. Yahweh is the God of all three generations simultaneously—and more!

The Family and the Church is the Church and the Family

In the last thirty years of being a pastor and ministry leader, I've witnessed a lot of attacks on families. Some are clearly the work of the evil one. Other attacks are the work of godless people and dynastic families that are antagonistic toward God.

And there is an attack on the church because the church today is much like the church recorded in the book of Acts; it is a family of families. We are part of God's family, and God is the head of our household. The church is the bride of Christ.

Something is interesting in the way God has established the church: he has done so with a structure in place that nearly all church folk understand—while Jesus is the head of the church, the church is led by elders (or deacons). And what are elders and deacons? The original root word and meaning in Greek is *grandfather*! Do you see it? Even in the church, there is an element of dynasty where many generations gather to worship and be in service to God.

The wisdom of placing elders (and/or deacons) in positions of influence is understood when we realize those who are older, have been following Jesus for years, have their own oikos in order,[4] and are (mostly) no longer seeking significance. They have enjoyed the satisfaction of their work and their family, and they are now transitioning from seeking personal significance to solidifying their legacy. For elders, instead of scrutinizing their own performance, they have the freedom to discern the health of the congregation and its ministry both inside and out.

The church is meant to be a family of families designed to support families. Why? Because God ordained the spiritual oikos to be the vehicle of equipping the called. But the family oikos is the primary place for raising sons and daughters. Sometimes we get that mixed up. We think pastors and churches are called to raise sons and daughters. But sons and daughters are not intended to be raised in any structure other than family. Why? Because heirship is not taught, it's caught. If you think the church is meant to do that, you have to have everybody in the church move in with the pastor. (And barring your church buying the $250 million home that is probably still on the market, I can guarantee you there is not enough room in their house for all of us to move in!)

This is part of the dominion mandate; we are to multiply. Just as God multiplied his family through Abraham, Isaac, and Jacob, and the twelve sons of Jacob, we too are to birth children into God's family. And it is the purpose of the Great Commission: we are to make disciples. The most effective way for families to make disciples is in the home and with the support of the church.

The family is meant to be the primary means of creating disciples, which is raising sons and daughters who follow Jesus.

The cultural idea that it takes a village to raise a child is partially true. More accurate is the idea that it takes multiple generations to raise a child, in both natural and spiritual families.

When we moved to Huntington in 2021, something profound happened to our son Jayden. He was growing spiritually because some amazing young leaders in our church—our spiritual oikos—reached out to him and engaged with him. Furthermore, some of the men in the church become mentors, echoing what his mom, Trudie, and I were teaching him. We celebrate our partnership with the church. It is integral to our success as we build our dynastic house. We are building our oikos, but we partner with the spiritual oikos; and together we will see the generation being raised, equipped, mandated, and prepared to fulfill God's kingdom purpose. Together we are bringing forth sons and daughters to love and serve our God.

Biblical Families

Christian families are those where the husband and wife submit to the lordship of Jesus Christ and train their children to follow him. Christian marriage is foundational to the Christian family. (Though, understandably, not every Christian family is currently led by a Christian husband and wife due to divorce, separation, or death. Christian marriage is not a mandatory prerequisite for a Christian family, but rather the intended foundation.)

The Bible teaches us about the nature of Christian families and how they function:

- Ephesians 5:22-26 – Provides guidelines for husbands and wives.
- Ephesians 6:4 – Instructs fathers to train their children in the Lord.
- 1 Timothy 5:8 – Explains it is the father's duty to provide for his family.
- Proverbs 31 – Demonstrates the virtues of a godly wife and the significance of the matriarch.
- Genesis 2:18-20 – Explains God gave man a woman to be a helpmate and to bear children.
- Ephesians 6:1-3 – Requires that children obey and honor their parents.
- Malachi 2:16 – Reveals that God hates divorce.
- Exodus 20:12 – Encourages children to "honor your mother and father."
- Luke 18:20 – Exhorts men and women to not commit adultery.
- Proverbs 17:6 – Revels in the fact that "grandchildren are

the crowning glory of the aged; parents are the pride of their children" (NLT).
- Malachi 4:6 – Declares that God will "turn the hearts of the parents to their children, and the hearts of the children to their parents."

As Trudie and I have journeyed with numerous families doing our life's work, we have observed an unexpected fruitfulness—we have seen many prodigal children come home! Why? Because once the father's house is in order, the father's heart is ready to celebrate what the prodigal adds to the dynastic purpose of the family and their generational purpose. When the father can begin to celebrate who God created them to be—their creativity and the gifting—many prodigals repent of their wandering ways and return to the family and their faith.

When parents are no longer standing against their children, with the Bible between them, but are saying, "You belong here because you are flesh of my flesh, bone of my bone," many children come home. When God turns our hearts to our children, that softened stance invites our children to turn their hearts toward us (see Malachi 4:6).

Our children and your children are born into a family to be part of God's dynastic mandate for that family. Each Christian child has spiritual gifts that can be exercised within the family to further the unique mission of the family. Every child, having been made in the image of God, has talents, interests, and giftings they can contribute to the family's mission. It is up to Christian parents to provide the necessary leadership and invite conversation about what the family mission and future will look like serving together.

We've experienced it with our own children, and I've experienced it with my brothers' families. By prioritizing the mandate of our family, which is in response to God's blessing (remember, in the five parts of the dominion mandate, the blessing comes first), we have been experiencing incredible healing and restoration. Various members of our families are embracing their purpose. We're building something profound together!

God Desires to Restore Broken Families

If you came out of a dysfunctional family situation, what's the greatest longing in your life? To be in a family. And often, they desire to be back in your family. I have often counseled both adopted and foster children, and one of the biggest dreams they have is to reconnect with their biological parents. They want to know who they are. Why? Because God has created this compulsion within the heart of humanity.

God wants to give back what the enemy stole. And he wants to build a new house because the glory of the latter house is going to be greater than the glory of the first house.

We know we are meant to belong to a family. And we know that together we are meant to do something beyond what we could ever imagine doing on our own. It's bigger than any one person.

The Malachi 4:6 passage above, so often translated as "turn their hearts to," is the restoration and reconciliation of relationships. This is the very heart of God. He desires to restore and reconcile people to himself.

Perhaps the pinnacle of the Bible, the story of the prodigal son in Luke 15, reveals the heart of God more than any other. Because God's love for us is about us, most of us see ourselves in this story as the younger son who rebuked his father, turned away from God, and in a moment of desperation, crawled back to him.

However, the key to this passage—and I suggest you spend ample time reading, enjoying, meditating on, and studying it—is the way God's heart for his children is revealed in the love of the father. The way Timothy Keller describes the prodigal father's heart posture toward his son is incredible: "I'm not going to wait until you've paid off your debt; I'm not going to wait until you've duly groveled. You are not going to earn your way back into the family, I am simply going to take you back. I will cover your nakedness, poverty, and rags with the robes of my office and honor."[5] Isn't that powerful?

We see the mockery he is willing to endure while waiting for and pursuing both his wayward and his dutiful children. And we see celebration when the lost child comes home.

Well before the genealogy of Jesus was given to us at the start of the New Testament (Matthew 1:1-17), God had been at work redeeming families. (Even the House of David, into which Jesus was born, has an adulterous, murderous, and scandalous past!)

Allow me to remind you of the call of Abraham and the promise God made to him and, by extension, to us—because as people of faith in Christ, it's a covenant that God is still fulfilling today:

> *"I will make you into a great nation,*
> *and I will bless you;*
> *I will make your name great,*
> *and you will be a blessing.*
> *I will bless those who bless you*
> *and whoever curses you I will curse;*
> *and all peoples on earth*
> *will be blessed through you."*
> *(Genesis 12:1-3)*

God did not tell Abraham he would be a blessing to just him and his family—but also to the whole world through Abraham's oikos. And what a household it was!

Abraham and Sarah didn't believe God when he said, "This man will not be your heir, but a son who is your own flesh and blood will be your heir" (Genesis 15:4). Having concluded that Sara was too old to get pregnant and have a child, Abraham, by Sara's suggestion, slept with Hagar, one of the servants in the house, who gave birth to Ishmael (Genesis 16:1-4). But not long after, Sara did get pregnant and gave birth to God's chosen heir Isaac.

But Isaac followed his father's fearful and deceitful ways and lied about being married to Rebekah to save his own life (see the accounts of Abraham in Genesis 12 and Isaac in Genesis 26).

And Jacob, the son of Isaac, deceived his father and stole his older brother's birthright with the help of his mother Rebekah (Genesis 27:35). Then, fearing for his life because of what he'd done to his brother Esau, he left his family to stay alive.

But God, still faithful through it all, called himself the God of Abraham, Isaac, and Jacob. He redeemed this family and blessed not only them but the entire nation of Egypt under the leadership of Joseph—Jacob's youngest son.

In the Old Testament, the people only knew God as God. Abraham, Isaac, Jacob, Joseph, and all of the tribes of Israel (one giant family of families) sought to bless the nations because that is what God told them to do.

Then, in the New Testament, Jesus came as a true representation of the Father—God in the flesh! And in Jesus, we see a perfect relationship between a father and a son. This is the first time God reveals himself as a father. He is the father of Jesus, and he is our Father in heaven.

In Jesus, God delivers the solution to the curse that stems from the fall and the curse that bludgeoned Abraham's family. He brings people together. God turns the hearts of moms and dads to their children and the hearts of children to their moms and dads. The spirit of God is a spirit of reconciliation.

One of the implications of being forgiven is that we now can forgive too. Just as Jesus, while suffering and dying on the cross, prayed: "Father, forgive them, for they do not know what they are doing" (Luke 23:34), we too, even while we are persecuted and suffering, can seek reconciliation and forgiveness. If you belong to Christ, you are part of the family of Abraham, and you are blessed. That's the promise! And part of the blessing is that you are forgiven of your sins.

As I reflect on my own heart and recall the stories of many members of the congregation we pastored in Austria, those who fought against apartheid in South Africa, and many who seek reconciliation in the political climate of the United States today, I am confident the two most difficult places to find reconciliation are within the family and the church. Some point to the myriad of broken relationships. Others point to unmet expectations, abusive legalism, or pastors who view themselves as the second coming of Christ and are bent on building their own empire. But the real reason reconciliation within families (and the church) seems harder than anywhere else is because these are the places of our deepest relationships. These are the places where the deepest relationships often lead to the deepest pain. It is also where sanctification occurs, and sanctification always involves molding, shaping, and cleansing—and it hurts! Reconciliation often requires a great deal of time, energy, humility, and grace to overcome our deepest pain. But there is hope because our capacity for reconciliation is defined by our relationship with God. And our relationship with God is defined by our having been created in his image, our belonging to Christ, and our belonging to his family—the church. It is through this relational capacity with God that we can bless the nations and bring the reconciling hope of Jesus Christ to those who join the family.

One of my lifelong joys is to care for and mentor young men who are growing in the faith. One of my great joys is the transformational story of the Walcher Family, the highlight of which was when I baptized both father and son at the same time.

The Walcher Family

Many skiing enthusiasts likely know the Walcher family from Austria, the one into which Jörg was born. Celebrated as world-class athletes, their family life, for many years, was nothing of the sort.

When Jörg was just a little boy, his famed grandfather died in a skiing accident in their hometown. When he was twelve, his father Heribert started drinking again after five years of abstinence. The family's following years were marked by severe depression, drugs and alcohol, his parent's divorce, the sale of his parent's hotel due to excessive debt, and the disintegration of all family ties. His heart hardened toward his father. He wanted nothing more to do with him or the family name.

A decade later, his mother—always faithful—invited him to attend a church service where a former surfer from South Africa (yours truly) was preaching. Moved by something he did not yet fully understand, Jörg said to Jesus, "If you really exist, then come into my heart and my life is yours." The power of God was overwhelming. He was seized by God's love and freedom. And he thought of his father.

In the days and weeks that followed, he began reading the Bible. One morning, he felt like he had to call his father and did. His dad was in the middle of heart complications and collapsed while they were on the phone.

Arriving at the hospital, Jörg learned the doctors had little hope for his father. He put his hands on his father's chest and prayed for him. The next day he brought headphones and had his dad listen to a reading of the Bible. Five days later, Jörg's father put his faith in Jesus Christ. Five weeks later the senior doctor said his father's x-ray looked like there had never been anything wrong. Very weak and frail, Heribert was ready to leave the hospital, but his road to recovery was to be a long one.

Although divorced for thirteen years, Jörg's mother, having had her own conversations with God, committed to live with her ex-husband and care for him during his recovery. There was nothing for her to gain, no family attachments, or emotional or financial blessing. She was motivated only by the loving mercy of God.

Weeks later, Heribert was free from depression and no longer drinking. Because of their time together, their love was renewed and the family was restored. In 2002, his parents married for the second time, and Jörg was the best man at his parent's wedding.

Today, Jörg and his wife, Jacqueline, are sports chaplains with Beyond Gold.[6] They care for professional athletes around the globe and lead church gatherings at the Olympic Games and various national competitions. They are the living fruit of God's work to re-story one broken family.

Now, inspired by God's work in and through the Walcher family, I want you to hear from Trudie, in her own words, how God blesses the nations through his many families, including yours.

Blessing to the Nations

Sean and I have always had a heart for the church and church planting. Together, we've always had a heart for the kingdom of God, which extends beyond the four walls of the church. And we've always been involved in business. Also, I dipped my hand into the political arena when we were in Australia. My desire to be part of transforming the political culture in Australia was birthed out of the political change I was a part of in South Africa. Sean and I were part of a movement that sought to reconcile people throughout the nation. We were part of a team at our church that held cultural gatherings in the early 1990s, before the election of Nelson Mandela as president (the first black president in South Africa). We were part of the team hosting symposiums on the biblical reconstruction of a nation.

World leaders and national news outlets said it was a miracle there wasn't a bloodbath in the whole election process. But they had no idea what God was doing behind the scenes. They had no idea that Christians were praying throughout the nation. And they had no idea how there was incredible reconciliation happening between races. At many of these meetings, we had people from different cultures come to the front and ask for forgiveness. We followed Jesus' biblical example to model humility to each other by washing each other's feet. It was an incredible movement of God! I get goosebumps every time I think about it—how God was bringing the country together. And how Christians came together with one voice, crying out to God for his deliverance, and seeking his plan for our nation.

In this movement, we were exposed to a kingdom message that Christians must be involved in culture and politics. If we didn't, we would be leaving decisions of life and death to the liars of this world. Then, when everything goes haywire, which it will, what would we do? We would stand and lament as we observed cities being burned and babies being killed. And we would complain that something should have been done to protect the people and prevent injustice.

I want to ask you, was Joseph (the son of Jacob and great-grandson of Abraham) a church leader, or was he a political leader? Remember, God has promised to bless the nations through his children. So, if you are called into business—praise the Lord that you're going to be a Christ follower in business. Do you want to work in education or media? Praise God because we need Christians to wield influence in these important spheres too. You can do so confidently because you carry the blessing of God wherever you go!

Joseph's Journey

Most of us know the biblical story of Joseph. We know how he was Jacob's favorite, was sold into slavery by his brothers, was put in jail for a sin he did not commit, and by God's power and grace, rose to the ranks of leadership in Egypt with power second only to the pharaoh himself. But why? Let us look at the blessing Jacob spoke over Joseph.

> *"Joseph is a fruitful vine,*
>   *a fruitful vine near a spring,*
>   *whose branches climb over a wall.*
> *With bitterness archers attacked him;*
>   *they shot at him with hostility.*
> *But his bow remained steady,*
>   *his strong arms stayed limber,*
> *because of the hand of the Mighty One of Jacob,*
>   *because of the Shepherd, the Rock of Israel,*
> *because of your father's God, who helps you,*
>   *because of the Almighty, who blesses you*
> *with blessings of the skies above,*
>   *blessings of the deep springs below,*
>   *blessings of the breast and womb."*

(Genesis 49:22-25)

Joseph was fruitful, not only in the vineyard but outside of its walls as well. He was persecuted by those who hated him. Yet God had a powerful plan for him. Dare I say, God gave him a mandate for his life. Joseph remained strong because of the mighty hand of his father upon him. It was God's promise to Jacob, and his blessing upon Joseph, that caused him to rise to power in Egypt. And he used this power to bless others! Through Joseph's knowledge and God's favor, the families of Israel, along with the people of Egypt, survived a seven-year famine. God "causes his sun to rise on the evil and the good, and sends rain on the righteous and the unrighteous" (Matthew 5:45). Sometimes, God does this through his family of families who are told to be fruitful, multiply, fill the earth, and establish dominion.

Every family history has its share of blessings and curses. Joseph's family sure did. David's family did. But God is a God of reconciliation, and his love stirs his mercy. As I look at my family history, we have experienced the curse of original sin and the curse of being opposed to the people of God. But the blessings God has given to my ancestors—because of his love modeled in and through Jesus Christ—are abundant! You can't even compare the two. It is important to appreciate that the curse is to the fourth generation and the blessing is to the $1,000^{th}$ generation. God's blessing is mathematically 250 times more impactful than the curse

We are not talking about blessing as if it is merely abundance, personal prosperity, or financial wealth. We are acknowledging that God's blessing is the fullness of his presence to empower us to do that which he commands. At the time of creation, God was the King ruling over his kingdom, and he blessed Adam and Eve with his lordship and power to carry out his commands. At the time of the Great Commission, Jesus promised his presence, the Holy Spirit, would be the dunamis through which he would carry out his command. The fruit of this blessing is always to the glory of God! And it is also for God's children and those who are yet to come to him.

Do not confuse the lies of this world with the truth of God. While God has a plan to prosper us and not to harm his children (Jeremiah 29:11), we know this is not a guarantee of health and wealth. (See the biblical stories of Joseph, Daniel, Esther, Stephen, and Paul, just to name a few.)

The Graham Family

Any conversation of family dynasty in America must include the Graham family. The multi-generational spiritual influence of this family has spanned the globe and reached into governments for decades.

The famed Reverend Billy Graham is renowned for his presence and preaching at more than 400 stadium-sized crowds in 185 countries on six continents. (And notably, at least to this author, in 1973, he shared the good news of Jesus Christ with more than 100,000 people at an event in Durban, South Africa.) It is estimated that he preached to more than two billion people at events and via radio and television broadcasts. Often referred to as "America's Pastor," he provided pastoral counsel to twelve consecutive presidents, from Harry S. Truman to Barack Obama.

But perhaps even more important than his own labors is the work of the Lord that continues to flourish in his absence. Graham's children have embraced God's call of the dominion mandate with the same fervor as their parents.

Franklin Graham continues his father's legacy as the CEO of the Billy Graham Evangelistic Association. He also serves as the president of Samaritan's Purse, which mobilizes the efforts of Christians in "providing spiritual and physical aid to hurting people around the world" and focuses on meeting the needs of "people who are victims of war, poverty, natural disasters, disease, and famine to share God's love through his Son, Jesus Christ."[7]

Anne Graham Lotz, Billy's daughter, has embraced her identity as a messenger of the Gospel. She is a prolific author, and she founded

AnGeL Ministries to "serve God by evangelizing the lost and reviving the hearts of God's people in their relationship with Himself through exalting Jesus Christ and proclaiming God's Word."[8]

Furthering the Graham family dynasty and the breakthrough of the kingdom of God in this world are Rachel-Ruth, the daughter of Anne, and William, the son of Franklin. Rachel-Ruth is part of AnGeL ministries, is involved in the Fellowship of Christian Athletes (FCA), and has followed in her mom's footsteps as an author. William is the executive director of the Billy Graham Training Center and is the third generation of the Graham family to preach under the banner of the Billy Graham Evangelistic Association.

More and more could be said about the children, grandchildren, and great-grandchildren of Billy and Ruth Graham. And frankly, you should read and listen to what they are saying to the world![9]

Reflection Questions

1. The Greek word oikos is exciting. It provides the foundation for spiritual growth and development for members of the family. Explain how your home serves as this type of foundation. Give examples.
2. There are two elements to the oikos—a family household and a spiritual household. Take a moment to assess which has a stronger influence on your life. How has God used it to shape your life?
3. In the Old Testament, we see the creation of the first dynastic family in the Abrahamic Covenant (Genesis 12:1-3), and this covenant is affirmed and reaffirmed numerous times in the book of Genesis. The key for God's people, from generation to generation, is to faithfully follow God as Lord. Are you nurturing covenant faithfulness in your family? If so, how?
4. What is the biggest benefit you see in celebrating a partnership with the church to build a dynastic family?

5. The Bible gives clear, strong guidance on how a Christian family functions. (A summary is detailed on page 84-85.) What do you see as the most helpful to your personal faith journey and that of your family?
6. What does it mean for you *to confidently carry the blessing of God wherever you go*? How might this influence your daily routine?

8
FAMILY IS THE VEHICLE FOR GOOD OR BAD

*But if serving the L*ORD *seems undesirable to you, then choose for yourselves this day whom you will serve, whether the gods your ancestors served beyond the Euphrates, or the gods of the Amorites, in whose land you are living. But as for me and my household, we will serve the L*ORD.

~ Joshua 24:15

Destroying family is not about destabilizing society. It's far more transcendent. You have to understand that the enemy knows what God sets in motion—God said dominion would come through dynasty. Satan knows there is a spiritual plan that has been set in motion, and he is fighting against it. He is working to undermine the efforts of Christian households, Christian families, and the Christian church to build dynasty. In many ways, he has been succeeding.

Imagine his response to the Protestant Reformation. I can imagine him saying, "Whoa, whoa, whoa! We can't have the families and their households following God and making a difference in the world." So, what did he do? He lied. He distorted. He enticed families to serve themselves. And we have the emergence of what is considered the 200 (or so) wealthiest families, who many believe rule the world.

I've researched the origin and function of many of these families. In most cases, they started with an individual who realized their capacity to influence the world, and they recorded their intent to build a dynasty. Where did that come from? Most of them were unbelievers. And they carried a secular, worldly agenda, which Satan used to his advantage.

Some thirty years ago, I had an economics professor of macroeconomics. He was a great teacher! Every time at the end of his class, he would say, "Just remember this: dynasties rule the world, not macroeconomics; dynasties have dictated the march of history." We all thought he was offering another one of his conspiracy theories—turns out he wasn't!

When I started learning about the dominion mandate, I realized I had initially failed to connect the two—the dominion mandate and family dynasties. God was grabbing my attention, and I started to see it: the enemy knows if he can stop the church from supporting and building dynastic households, he will continue to build his dynasty and keep his grip on the world.

Five Arrows

One of the most famous families in history is the Rothschilds, who rose to prominence under the leadership of Mayer Amschel Rothschild (1744-1812), who began to finance the purchase of assets after having learned to trade in coins, artifacts, and collectibles. He had five sons whom he brought into the business.

The business started small, as most do, and it grew quickly. He leveraged his business success and moved into banking to aid those who needed a loan, and he did so with tremendous integrity, offering low-interest loans and, in some cases, unsecured loans. He created a credit structure to ascertain the risk associated with the loans. Discovering that more and more people needed help, he trained his sons and sent them to five European cities: London, Paris, Frankfurt, Vienna, and Naples.

The family crest boasts the values *Concordia, Integritas, Industria* (Latin for "Harmony, Integrity, Industry") and depicts a single hand holding five arrows (one for each of the sons). Where does this come from? Perhaps this family dynasty at least acknowledges their family lineage and sees the truth in the Scriptures of the Jews:

> *"Children are a heritage from the Lord,*
> *offspring a reward from him.*
> *Like arrows in the hands of a warrior*
> *are children born in one's youth.*
> *Blessed is the man*
> *whose quiver is full of them.*
> *They will not be put to shame*
> *when they contend with their opponents in court."*
> (Psalm 127:3-5)

I do not know the faith of the members of this Jewish family, but I can say that at some point in time, they took their God seriously. The Rothschilds clearly function as a dynasty; that is, they embrace the dominion mandate as a family (as stated in chapter two), identify their family name and mission, engage children and grandchildren with a seat at the table, grow their capacity to exercise their rule, create an environment in which each member can thrive, and influence their communities. Whether they are doing so for their own glory or God's is yet to be seen.

Why Not in the Church?

Why has this not been done in the church? What would the world look like today if the church had been—for millennia—supporting families in pursuit of their mission and mandate? How might the kingdom of God and his holiness have broken through in recent centuries? What would our worship, service, and giving look like? What would our communities, schools, and businesses look like? Empowering families within God's church is crucial!

Thankfully, it is a new day, and we have declared war on the enemy. Christian families need to behave like Mayer Rothschild and focus on building a family dynasty, creating wealth, and generating influence. We need to develop a mindset of building and not consuming and spending. We need to move beyond our petty selfishness and irreverent individualism. We need to stop being enticed by the lies of the world.

When we develop a dynastic mindset, we initiate the butterfly effect. The slightest change, the smallest correction, can have a tremendous impact three, four, or five generations from now! It's not enough to leave your family better off, prepare the next generation for success, or save the world for your grandchildren.

Christians are to become the pillars of the community on which all goodness stands.

> *The essence of dynastic families is to manifest and make known the dominion of God and his goodness to all people, to the glory of God, and for the benefit of believers and non-believers everywhere!*

We have to approach this mindset with a spirit of servanthood. Again, the dominion mandate is not about compelling or forcing others to submit to your authority. Rather, it is about using God's mandate to bring blessings to others. There is no place in the Christian heart for lording over others. Like Jesus, we are called to serve.

Have you noticed that you hardly hear about the Rothschilds? This family epitomizes the ideal of conducting *everything in obscurity to ensure security*. They value not only their privacy but also their meekness. They have the sword (or quiver of arrows) but rarely remove it from its sheath. You will never hear about with whom they meet. You won't see them on a list of Hollywood stars. And any effort to quantify their family wealth can only be loosely estimated in billions or trillions because no one has access to research the magnitude of their family dynasty.

So, again, I ask, why not in the church? Thankfully, faithful men and women are discovering their God-given purposes and re-storying their families. My good friends Mat and Janice are doing this very thing today and have joined the Family Dynasty team.

The Dewing Family

They would not have considered themselves a dynasty, yet they have faithfully stewarded a 500-acre generational farm in northeastern Pennsylvania for five generations. Andy and Sally Dewing are now the patriarch and matriarch living on and operating the family farm. In their generation, they have successfully transitioned from four generations of dairy farming to now producing maple syrup, high-quality grass-fed beef, and a stone quarry.

They raised three boys on the farm, and, as of this writing, have seventeen grandchildren, five grandchildren-in-law, and four great-grandchildren. Two of the three sons have built their own beautiful timber frame homes on the land almost entirely from resources on the farm. Their third son owns another farm close by where his family lives. The entire family enjoys doing life together in much the same way their ancestors needed to for basic survival.

Every Sunday afternoon, Andy and Sally prepare a feast for whoever might choose to drop by after church. On any given Sunday, the gathering might only be ten people for lunch, or quite possibly twenty-five.

As enjoyable as the Sunday gatherings are, it is the monthly Family Table Meeting no one wants to miss. Every family member over the age of thirteen has a seat at the table, and these days for the Dewing family that means twenty-four of them.

Over the past year as the family has awakened to God's design for families to live intentionally with a dynastic framework and vision, they have rejoiced in the rich legacy, which generations before have deposited and stewarded. By faith, they believe God has awakened them to another level of stewardship that will bring about presently unknown future flourishing to generations of family members and communities that God takes the Dewing house into.

In recent years, through the process of mining family redemptive blessings, the Dewing family embraced their clear mandate from God to protect and steward with humility. This has provided clarity, focus, and a sense of purpose for the family. The mandate is specific enough to help them stay on point, yet broad enough to have staying power through as many future generations as God allows.

Although the Dewing family has enjoyed strong, devoted, honoring relationships, through this dynastic awakening and reframing, there has emerged a renaissance of individual and collective excitement, purpose, and hope. In past years, various family members had succeeded in their respective business ventures, but the family had not previously envisioned the power of working together on a legacy business that would be the foundation for future generations. They have counted the cost and are willing to persevere through the inherent challenges of mentoring and being mentored beyond the parenting years.

The Dewings are excited to see how God allows their surrendered plans to bless the world. They have a deep conviction that God has, in this generation, called them to live in a way that is multiplicative, not just additive. They are changing estate plans that would have before divided the inheritance but will now consolidate the inheritance for the exponential flourishing of future generations.

Dynastic Families

If you were to study the 200 most influential men, women, and families in the world, you would discover, as I have, that they all function as dynasties. Even contemporaries such as Elon Musk (Tesla/X), Mark Zuckerberg (Facebook/Meta), Michael Green (Hobby Lobby), and Dan Cathy (Chick-fil-A) are bolstered by the dynastic decision-making (intentional or not) of their forefathers.

These families have many qualities in common: They identify a narrow mission that the family will pursue even while supporting the assignments and talents of individual family members. They make the business of the family the family business. They vet possible spouses to ensure alignment with the family's mission. They work diligently to create wealth, primarily through real estate and intellectual property. And when something goes wrong in the family, the family fixes it.

We have all seen the family drama of the House of Windsor play out in the public eye in recent years. When Prince Harry decided to marry Meghan Markle, it was done only with the consent of the family, albeit a painful one. And when they determined it was best for them to separate from the responsibility of being part of the Royal Family, it was done with the agreement of the family. It is widely known that Prince Harry had a wonderful relationship with his grandmother, Queen Elizabeth, even while having a strained relationship with the throne; for tension exists not in the personal relationship but in the embracing of his seat at the table.

It is, of course, tragic that we "peasants" are witness to the plight of the Royal Family. It reminds us that something is not right in the world. (Or maybe it makes us feel a little better about the family struggles we experience?) But more important than the painful and embarrassing family discord in London at the time of this writing, is the painful misalignment of Christian families around the globe who are not aligned with the will of the one who sits at the right hand of God.

Heirs with Christ

As Christians, we are the *huios* (mature sons and daughters) of God. That is, as sons and daughters, we have full legal standing as a member of God's family. The Apostle Paul teaches in Romans 8:14-17 that we are heirs with Christ:

> For those who are led by the Spirit of God are the children of God. The Spirit you received does not make you slaves, so that you live in fear again; rather, the Spirit you received brought about your adop-

tion to sonship [huios]. And by him we cry, "Abba, Father." The Spirit himself testifies with our spirit that we are God's children. Now if we are children, then we are heirs—heirs of God and co-heirs with Christ, if indeed we share in his sufferings in order that we may also share in his glory.

We are the sons and daughters of the Living King. By the work of Christ and the power of the Holy Spirit, we can carry the authority of God wherever we go. Why? Because we are united in Christ, who has proclaimed the will of his Father: "All authority in heaven and on earth has been given to me (Matthew 28:18). Allow me to ask; if Jesus has *all authority*, how much do we have? We have none! What we have is the blessing of God. And we carry the message of God. We can exercise Christ's authority through the working of the Holy Spirit in us and through us. But we also have the human will to choose not to—to be disobedient.

It is the power of God at work in us that empowers us to know the truth and act as children of God. It is the power of God that enables us to share in the sufferings of Christ and also in his glory. It is the power of the Spirit that enables us to carry the authority of God wherever we go and enact his life-giving and family-redeeming power in the world around us. We do this by heeding God's call on our lives. We do this by advancing the mission of our family dynasty for the sake of others. We do this by fulfilling our mandate within the context of the greater body of believers—the church. Remember, we belong in family, but greater still is the reality that we belong to Jesus!

The Spiritual House

God ordained the spiritual house, the oikodomé (suitably translated as *house of dome or rule*), to be a place of power and worship. He equipped his church as the spiritual house with the five-fold ministry: "So Christ himself gave the apostles, the prophets, the evangelists, the pastors, and teachers, to equip his people for works of service, so that the body of Christ may be built up until we all reach unity in the faith and in the knowledge of the Son of God and become mature, attaining to the whole measure of the fullness of Christ" (Ephesians 4:11-13). These five gifts of apostleship, prophecy, evangelization, pastoring, and teaching are the means through which the authority of Christ is carried to the world. This is done through the spiritual house—the church. When we view the equipping of the community of saints, alongside the giving of the dominion mandate to Adam and Eve, we see God intends that each of our families gathers under one place of leadership and support—the church, with Christ as the head—to bring about the fullness of the authority of Christ here on earth. And this is no small task.

In the last hundred years, there has been a boom of new Christian organizations serving people and communities around the globe. Parachurch organizations like Focus on the Family and Compassion International have flourished with worldwide reach through this new focus on collaborative service. While family dynasties were devolving, Christian ministries were developing (and parachurch Christian ministries sure do look a lot like biblical family dynasties). There seems to be a correlation between the absence of family dynasty and the increase in mission-minded, service-oriented organizations. It is as if, when families began abdicating their dominion mandate authority to the church, individual Christians created their own enterprises to live out their place of ruling in response to their calling.

Before anyone wonders where I am going with this, let it be known that I am an advocate for parachurch Christian ministries as they can go places and influence people in a way the church cannot. There is an economy of scale and collective effectiveness when like-minded individuals gather their spiritual, intellectual, and financial capital for the sake of the kingdom of God. To do so under the banner of an organization that professes the name of Jesus is a blessing to all. Still, I wonder if the advent of such organizations is the faithful work of God in response to the failings of families. That said, I believe that as families are restored, the family/parachurch/church partnership has the potential to take on a whole new dynamic!

God is at work advancing his kingdom, redeeming humanity, and creating and purposing families. Of this, there can be no doubt. God will always uphold his sovereignty as the King of Kings. He will forever maintain his covenant with his people. And he will continue to create and purpose families whom he will bless and through whom he can cause the world to flourish. But in the face of the destruction of the family, God continues to accomplish his will, albeit through this other, and perhaps, less permanent means.

I began this chapter by identifying the fight: Satan is working to undermine the efforts of Christian households, Christian families, and the Christian church to build dynasty and wield the authority of Christ on Earth. In many regards, he has been succeeding. But we should be encouraged because we can see that, while the culture around us deteriorates, the heart of God for his people and the power of the Holy Spirit continues to be revealed. Many faith-filled families act as signposts, standing at the crossroads, pointing us in the way we should go.

The Green Family

Perhaps less known than Billy Graham—yet no less notable—is David Green, an American businessman and the founder of Hobby Lobby Stores, Inc.—a chain of arts and crafts stores. Green is the son of a pastor, and each of his siblings is either a pastor or a pastor's wife. Various members of the Green family—children and grandchildren—serve throughout facets of the family business either within Hobby Lobby, at Mardel Christian & Education bookstores, or the family-funded Museum of the Bible in Washington, DC.

I have often said the *business of the family is the family business*, and the Greens are the quintessential example of this mantra. As a family, they are committed to "honoring the Lord in all we do by operating the company in a manner consistent with Biblical principles."[1]

How do they do this? They compensate their employees above market value and close their stores on Sundays to "allow employees time for family and worship." Their real estate investing plan focuses on leasing existing large commercial space within cities to revitalize stagnant economic regions (often referred to as in-filling), and they leverage their economic and social clout to defend the freedoms of the people in their communities. This has caused them to stand against immoral, unbiblical laws coming out of Washington, DC.

Like the Graham family, the Green family enthusiastically promotes the good news of Jesus throughout the world; they support Christian education and have given hundreds of millions of dollars to churches and parachurch Christian ministries, and they are sponsors of the YouVersion Bible app that makes the Bible available in more than 140 languages.[2] Additionally, they partner with Biblica (the International Bible Society),[3] to fund and encourage the open-source translation of the Bible in languages where the Bible has not yet been translated. Through the profits of Mardel, they invest in the printing and donating of Bibles translated by Wycliffe Bible Translators.[4] The impact of this family goes well beyond what we can see or experience personally.

But the family business was not always this way or this large. While it was David and Barbara Green who started what would become Hobby Lobby in 1970, with a $600 loan, it was David's father —a pastor—who had the vision to reach beyond the walls of a church and start a small family-owned business to fight poverty in his community. The elder Green employed most of his congregation, and as the seeds began to bloom, the perspective of the community was reframed, and hope began to flourish.

Praise be to God for the Green family and the ongoing ministry of Hobby Lobby, Mardel, the YouVersion Bible app, Biblica, and Wycliffe Bible Translators. I confess that sometimes it is difficult to assess where family dynasty ends and organizational ministry begins, but I am sure we don't need to spend any time delineating such an arbitrary concern because it is the will of God that we all live and function in the lordship of Jesus Christ. There is only one oikodomé under which all other oikoses live.

∽

Reflection Questions

1. Mayer Rothchild built a family dynasty by creating wealth and generating influence. This runs counter to the cultural trends of consuming and spending. How has your wealth and influence been influenced by your patterns of consumption and spending? Journal your thoughts.
2. As believers, we carry the authority of God wherever we go. This means we carry this family-redeeming power into the world around us. Consider what areas you are carrying this authority. How might you take this power into the lives of more people?
3. The spiritual house, oikodomé, is a place of power and worship. Each oikodomé carries the five gifts of apostleship, prophecy, evangelism, pastoring, and teaching. What minister has most influenced your life? Explain.
4. How is your family a spiritual signpost pointing others to the way they should go?

9
UNDER THE DOME

Now no shrub had yet appeared on the earth and no plant had yet sprung up, for the L<small>ORD</small> God had not sent rain on the earth and there was no one to work the ground . . .

~ Genesis 2:5

Historically, churches were built with an architectural dome because, in the ancient world, it declared the ultimate evidence that the religion had taken possession of the land and shifted the belief system and culture of its people. It implies dominion—the dominion of the kingdom. And this is why during periods of Islamic expansion following the war, they did not destroy the church buildings and cathedrals but reframed them to become mosques. It was their declaration of a new dominion (but in an uncontrolled manner). Today, the vast majority of mosques in the Middle East were originally cathedrals and churches.

Why all this talk about families being part of churches and churches being a family of families? Because when you are an heir in God's oikos—his household—you have a seat at the table. There is authority. There is partnership. There is responsibility. And when you start building your family dynastically, what does this imply? What does this mean? Well, what does the word *dome* sound like? Dominion. And that is exactly what it means. Our families are households under the authority of God with the capacity to enact dominion, which can be understood as service through exercising a controlled strength.

It parallels growing dominion through dynastic families. Think of it spiritually, and then think of it in the context of your family. We're right back to growing your family through the blessing of the dominion mandate given to Adam and Eve and, subsequently, all families.

When you choose to follow God, your oikos (your family or household) becomes a place of dominion in the kingdom of God. Your oikos is part of the natural and spiritual oikodomé that is the Body of Christ. And Jesus says there is nothing that will "prevail against" his kingdom and his church (Matthew 16:18). There is no demonic force that can come in and destroy your family, your children, your grandchildren, or your great-grandchildren when you are in Christ. As Christians, we belong to Christ, and it is from the victory of Christ on the cross that we wage war for the sake of the kingdom of God. It is in the authority of Christ that we battle against the spiritual forces that bring poverty to communities, divorce to homes, and oppress the widow and the orphan.

Every one of our families has the capacity for good or bad; it all comes down to where we root our oikos—either under the authority of Christ or under some false god. And every oikos, having been blessed by God with the transformative power to take dominion and to subdue, can do good or bad. Let me say this: there is no such thing as having an oikos without an intent to become part of an oikodomé. It's within its DNA. I think this is why kids often run off to find a place of belonging elsewhere when they don't find purpose and identity at home; it is in their DNA to find a place to live out God's calling on their lives. They want to be part of something bigger and more powerful than themselves that is influencing the world. They want to be part of building something of value. They want a place that allows them to express their gifting. (Does this sound anything like starting or joining a church or parachurch Christian organization?)

Dietrich's Way

It was 1926, and Dietrich Bonhoeffer, the German pastor and cultural transformer, was speaking to his preachers' seminary in Berlin. "He was quite aware of the secluded life of the seminary and the turmoil of Berlin outside its walls, where Fascists and Communists fought in the Streets."[1] Before turning his attention to Psalm 127, which begins with the familiar biblical axiom, "Unless the Lord builds the house, the builders labor in vain," Bonhoeffer implored his listeners:

> We live in a time when more than ever before we speak and must speak of building and rebuilding. We speak of how our commerce must grow and what trade agreements will bring about this result today or tomorrow, as quickly as possible. We speak of the best arrangements on workers' wages and how workers and employers alike can find a common interest in success. We ask ourselves how we can begin to become once more rich, trouble-free, happy and respected people. We work today as perhaps we have never worked before to achieve that goal as soon as possible . . . And we thank those men and women who dedicate themselves to this and do fruitful work. And every one of us here who would wish to belong to this band of men and women who take seriously love of their neighbor in this work.[2]

Bonhoeffer speaks of how Christians need to engage in society and respond to the human desire to influence people who are financially free and healthy in body and soul. He speaks of a social, moral building that begins with personal moral growth. He speaks of balancing work in the city with exploration, dancing, and playing in the countryside. Bonhoeffer, aware of the pain following World War I, envisioned a world in which people were flourishing. Then, he dropped the hammer: "Woe betide us if it is not so! Otherwise, we are truly only Sunday Christians from 9:00 to 10:00 in the morning!"[3]

Wow! Whether Jesus comes back tomorrow, one hundred years from now, or a millennium from now, he is going to find his people building. He will find dynastic families, and thousands of others, working out our faith in the pattern of Scripture. He will find us embracing our blessing, wielding our Holy Spirit power through dynasty, and taking dominion within his kingdom. He will find our children and our children's children, and our children's children's children doing the same. This is what he will find in the Morris oikos, as we will be a house of dominion for the Lord!

Your Family and the Oikodomé of God

Whether your family is a vehicle for good or bad is entirely up to you.

This is one of the major tensions of free will. We choose to love ourselves or to love God and others. What will you choose?

Many years ago, Trudie and I were attending a prayer meeting at our church. And as God often does, he showed up in a mighty way and brought clarity to Trudie on a topic that she had been asking about for some time— the truth of whom God made you and your family to be.

Having been made in the image of God and being blessed with the capacity to rule, you have to decide if you will rule under the authority of Jesus in the kingdom of God or if you will build your own little empire on earth.

I (Trudie) had been thinking about curses and blessings and wondering which was stronger. As my mind returned to that question, the Holy Spirit asked me to answer my own question. "Obviously, the blessing, Lord," I replied.

And the voice of God came back to me so quickly: "So, why are you spending so much time in your prayer meetings just praying for the problems in all the families and not embracing the blessing? The blessing is to 1,000 generations, and the curse is only to the fourth."

With that, I started a new journey of listening to the Lord about families, generations, and blessings.

Back in 2000, the world discovered a little book by Bruce Wilkinson titled *The Prayer of Jabez*. The namesake of the book is two verses found in 1 Chronicles 4, which record the history of the family of Abraham. The verses are the prayer of a man named Jabez, whose life was probably miserable because his name sounds like the Hebrew word for pain. These two verses echo the dominion mandate and foreshadow the Great Commission: "Jabez was more honorable than his brothers. His mother had named him Jabez, saying, 'I gave birth to him in pain.' Jabez cried out to the God of Israel, 'Oh, that you would bless me and enlarge my territory! Let your hand be with me, and keep me from harm so that I will be free from pain.' And God granted his request" (vs. 9-10).

More than nine million copies were sold. And Wilkinson's book started a movement! Some people found confidence in the presence of God in their lives, others foolishly embraced the teaching as a promise from God to fulfill all of their worldly desires, and others rejected it because it seemed a little too similar to the perverted teaching of the "health and wealth prosperity gospel" teaching of some inside the church. What the book did accomplish was to raise the awareness of many Christians about God's desire that we fulfill his mission to the ends of the earth in every way he has designed us to.

Jabez was very likely aware of the covenantal blessing that God made to Abraham—it's one that Jabez himself was part of. He prayed a beautiful prayer that acknowledged the power and presence of God in his life. Jabez had confidence in God. He talked with God in a way that caused many of us to read his words and pause. We think, "I can't talk to God like that!" But you can! We can come into the presence of our Father in heaven free of any guilt, condemnation, or unworthiness. That is what righteousness means. We are righteous before God because of Jesus! We are sons and daughters of the Most High King because the righteousness of Jesus has been imputed to all believers. In Christ, we have divine favor. We can ask God to bless us because God has already blessed us in Christ. In asking for our blessings, we are stating that we are confident in who God is, and we are ready to receive the blessing.

Jabez, this man of faith living under the covenant of Abraham, asked for a blessing. He prayed that God would "enlarge [his] territory," his family, his fruitfulness, and his reach. Then he pleaded with God to never let him go. Jabez wanted to *receive* God's blessing so he could *be* a blessing. Jabez wanted his life to be evidence of more of God and less of him. This is the fruit of the blessing that comes from living in the kingdom of God—the place where God has set up his rule and reign over our lives.

As a follower of Jesus, when we live under and submit to the authority of Christ, we want what he wants, which is ultimately what the Father wants; and we will choose to love God and love others more than we love ourselves. We will receive a blessing so we can be a blessing. We will receive God's love with a desire to give away his love.

The prayer of Jabez is reflective of the first part of becoming a family dynasty. It is a vehicle for good that God uses to help us understand that God loves and blesses us because he desires to love us and bless us. His love causes him to love us whether we are lovable or not. And his blessing is intended for us but is also to be delivered *through* us. It is reminiscent of the wisdom and intent of Solomon, who, when "God said, 'Ask for whatever you want me to give you,'" Solomon answered with, "So give your servant a discerning heart to govern your people and to distinguish between right and wrong" (1 Kings 3:1-15).

To become a family dynasty is to understand who you are and where you came from. In this process of stepping into where you came from, you will understand where you can go. It is relatively easy to discover our family lineage today, or at least the genetic identity we have, which we share with our forebarers. But what is more important than our genetic makeup is our God-given identity—our name and our heritage. We are going to look at these important facets of our identity together.

As you begin to examine your name and family and all of the good and bad throughout the generations, I implore you to focus on the goodness of God—on the blessing. (We call them the redemptive generational blessings.) This focus is a significant part of re-storying your family.

The enemy wants us to focus on the negative, to only see the part of our family that has done evil in the eyes of God. But God desires something more. He has redeemed us, and we can stand in his promise of blessing. What is this blessing we stand in? It is nothing less than the nature of God that creates our capacity to be like Jesus and to love others.

As Jabez embraced his part in God's covenant with Abraham, so must we. He prayed that God would enlarge his territory. And God has promised to do just that! Remember, the dominion mandate includes three stages: God's purpose, the strategy, and the victory. Enlarging your tent is part of the strategy. God is at work making it possible for us to be fruitful, increase in number, and fill the earth. He does this in every family, including yours.

I know God's hand is on my life because he leads me. He directs me. He shows me the way. He protects me. He takes me where he wants me to go because I am his. He has called me by my name, and I am his.

And if you are in Christ, by faith, so are you! This is where your identity—your name and heritage—comes from. There is no lie from the enemy that can pervert this truth. As you look at your family name and family heritage, do so with confidence in the One whose purpose is perfect, strategy is secure, and victory is guaranteed.

Your Family Name

There are countless books and websites and pseudo-professionals dedicated to helping moms and dads name their children. There is even a 2010 documentary film based on the book *Freakonomics*[4] that examines the implication of the power of culturally identifiable names in personal success and social engagement. Yet we need to understand that while we think we are just giving cute, trendy names to our children, they are pre-planned by God. He has named every one of us in the same way he named Jesus, which means "one who saves". Because our identity is in Jesus Christ (the name above every other name), our names are, likewise, in him and from him. And our family names have been given to us for a purpose so we can embrace our role in the dynastic breakthrough of the kingdom of God. We see it plainly in the Abrahamic covenant.

There is a remarkable revelation of the nature of God in the Abrahamic dynasty: God names and purposes individuals. Joseph, through whom God saved Jacob and his entire family, had a name that meant *to increase*. He named his sons Manasseh, which means *forget the past*, and Ephraim, which means *to be fruitful*. It seems God named and purposed Joseph and his sons, the fourth and fifth generations of his covenant with Abraham, to be the pivot point for the transformation of the household of Abraham to become the many tribes of Israel—the oikos became the foundation for the oikodomé.

It is no surprise to Sean and me that his family name Morris means "of the marsh," as his entire family line is rich in land ownership and agriculture.

What is your family name? What does it mean? And what blessing does it convey?

Your Family Blessing

If every dynastic family can be a blessing to the nations, what might that blessing be? In everything we do, we are to be the revelation of the character of God to the watching world. This is our mandate, and within it, we find our mission.

One of the more popular passages of Scripture is Jesus' Sermon on the Mount, which includes a list of blessings and an exhortation that we should be that blessing:

Now when Jesus saw the crowds, he went up on a mountainside and sat down. His disciples came to him, and he began to teach them.

The Beatitudes

He said:
"Blessed are the poor in spirit,
  for theirs is the kingdom of heaven.
Blessed are those who mourn,
  for they will be comforted.
Blessed are the meek,
  for they will inherit the earth.
Blessed are those who hunger and thirst for righteousness,
  for they will be filled.
Blessed are the merciful,
  for they will be shown mercy.
Blessed are the pure in heart,
  for they will see God.
Blessed are the peacemakers,
  for they will be called children of God.
Blessed are those who are persecuted because of righteousness,
  for theirs is the kingdom of heaven.
Blessed are you when people insult you, persecute you and falsely say all kinds of evil against you because of me. Rejoice and be glad, because great is your reward in heaven, for in the same way they persecuted the prophets who were before you."
(Matthew 5:1-12)

From the very beginning, God has purposed families to be his vehicle for transformation in this world. In these verses, Jesus clarifies what it looks like to enact that transformation.[5] While I do recommend that all of us spend time seeking the will of God through Jesus' words in his Sermon on the Mount, I want to draw your attention to one specific aspect of this powerful sermon. Jesus speaks not only to the transformation of the heart that occurs in every believer but also to the transformative power of the family of believers to reveal the character of God. This character is shaped in us when we apply the words of Jesus through our good deeds.

Jesus makes it clear we are not to hoard these blessings but to put them to good use. We are to use our blessings, our larger family, and our expanded territory—the blessings of God—for a purpose. And what is that purpose? We are to be salt and light.

> "You are the salt of the earth. But if the salt loses its saltiness, how can it be made salty again? It is no longer good for anything, except to be thrown out and trampled underfoot."
>
> "You are the light of the world. A town built on a hill cannot be hidden. Neither do people light a lamp and put it under a bowl. Instead, they put it on its stand, and it gives light to everyone in the house. In the same way, let your light shine before others, that they may see your good deeds and glorify your Father in heaven."
> (Matthew 5:13-16)

For some, this may be too stark of a warning to come from the mouth of Jesus, but in the same way salt can lose its saltiness, so too can the church, families, and individuals lose the power of their testimony before man. That is not to say they can lose their salvation, but it is to say we have a choice in whether we will use our capacity to serve God or to build our own empire. We can choose to remain a single nuclear family disconnected from the larger family of God, or we can partner with other families in the body of Christ to love our neighbors. We can choose to remain cloistered in our homes away from the pain of the world, or we can run onto the battlefield to save lives.

We, the Morris family, are choosing to carry the authority of Christ wherever we go to increase the blessing of God in the lives of everyone we know—to the glory of God alone! We want to be a blessing to others. We are embracing our God-given mandate to take dominion, not only because he told us to but because we share in his desire to bless people and save them from the attacks of the evil one. And frankly, the world is in so much pain because of so many self-absorbed dynasties that it is impossible for us not to seek to bring God's saving grace to a waiting world.

~

Reflection Questions

1. Dietrich Bonhoeffer exhorted Christians to engage society —especially those who are financially free and healthy in body and soul. He envisioned a world where people flourished! In what ways are you and your family contributing to the flourishing of others?
2. When Jesus returns, he will find dynastic families, and thousands of others, working our faith in the pattern of Scripture. In what ways will you and your family be working to wield your Holy Spirit power through dynasty? Through taking dominion within God's kingdom?
3. Have you decided to build your own empire or rule under the authority of King Jesus? Explain your understanding of both.
4. Living under the Abrahamic Covenant, the Old Testament figure Jabez prayed to God with a simple request, "enlarge my territory." Have you asked God to bless you so you might be a blessing to others? How have you seen God answer this prayer?
5. Do you know your family name? What is it? What does it mean?

10
DYNASTIC FAMILY BY DESIGN

"As for me, this is my covenant with them," says the Lord*. "My Spirit, who is on you, will not depart from you, and my words that I have put in your mouth will always be on your lips, on the lips of your children and on the lips of their descendants— from this time on and forever," says the* Lord*.*

~ Isaiah 59:21

Every biblical family dynasty that has ever been began with one person, or one couple, believing in God. Not only believing but trusting. Not only trusting but obeying. Not only obeying but building. And what do we believe? Nothing less than Christ's victory over death.

Without the resurrection of Christ, we would not have the assurance of eternal life (1 Corinthians 15:20-23), God's provision of the power to live in victory over sin (15:24-34), and the confidence that our labor is not in vain (15:50-58). But it is not merely our belief in the resurrection power of Jesus that gives us power; it is the lordship of Jesus and our adoption as sons and daughters, rightful heirs, that does so. It is the presence of the Spirit of God in our lives that enables us to live as the workmanship of God and to fulfill our dominion mandate as dynastic families.

I readily admit, as a pastor and theologian, I can get caught up in the grand story of God, working to realize his dream that we all live in the too-good-to-be-true fairytale story he is writing for all of us. I can see it woven throughout the pages of the greatest love story ever written: from Adam and Eve to Noah, to Abraham, Isaac, and Jacob, to David, and from Jerusalem to Judea, Samaria, and the ends of the earth. I delight in how God reveals himself so plainly to us, making the seemingly incomprehensible so simply knowable. And while the story of the Bible is truly all about him, I also know it has much to do with you, your family, and your neighbors.

As we have realized before, the story of the Bible contains great themes of Scripture: the kingdom of God, the love of God, and God's purpose in creating families. Why did God create families? Why are we called children of God? So we can express the love of God in his kingdom. We have done that extraordinarily well throughout the ages, and we must continue to do so because, as S. Michael Craven so well synthesizes in his book *Uncompromised Faith: Overcoming our Culturalized Christianity*,

> From virtual obscurity, Christianity rose to challenge and conquer one of the greatest empires the world has ever seen: the Roman Empire. Christianity served to civilize and educate an entire continent; it gave birth to modern ideals of freedom, human dignity, equality, free market economics, and social justice. Christianity forever established as universal human virtues the concepts of compassion, love, sacrifice, and forgiveness. The monuments of Christianity can still be seen everywhere: from the cathedrals of Europe to the music of Bach; from the intellectual heritage of Augustine, Aquinas, and Calvin to the literature of Dante, Milton, and Shakespeare. From the colonization of America to the abolition of slavery, Christianity has been the most powerful and, one might add, most positive formative influences on culture in the history of the world.[1]

Some contend that Christians should live in the world but not engage in it—that we should not make an effort to transform the kingdoms of this world because we are made for another world. Imagine if our spiritual ancestors thought that same way. Where would we be now? Would you and I be following Jesus today? Would we be gathering for corporate worship in local churches? Would we have Christian charities serving orphans and widows? Would we be promoting the value of every life? Would women and children be honored members of society? Would slavery still be the worldwide atrocity it once was?

In the next couple of chapters, we will step into your part of the story of God and how you and your family can embrace his calling on your lives to fulfill the mandate to exercise dominion by becoming a family that lives dynastically. And by identifying your family's identity and purpose, you will learn how to re-story your family for the sake of Christ and bless your community (if not the nations).

Let's begin with a look at how our family is becoming a dynastic family and then walk through the seven steps necessary to embrace the fullness of what God has in store for your family and those you will bless.

The House of Morris

For two generations, the Morris family forgot the Lord.

Both from the passing down of family lore and through our own research, I know the House of Morris has been a generational family that worked the land as farmers and vineyard owners. Throughout most of the generations, it was rarely to our benefit: three times our family funded the construction of a church building and paid the salary of the pastor; and our family would regularly employ the citizens of the region with integrity and purpose. The House of Morris lived out their family purpose, perhaps not dynastically, but clearly from generation to generation. But then, two generations of family patriarchs and matriarchs lost their way, and their hearts gravitated toward the world and away from God.

Assuming the mantel of the family business and acknowledging the squabbling over would-be inheritances, my father Rod Morris felt the weight of the demand to succeed. Feeling the burden and pressure, he cried out to God, and it was in this temporal pain that my dad began to walk faithfully with the Lord. With a new perspective—a growing "mind of Christ" view of the world—he examined his place in the family line. He recognized the light of the family legacy was dimmed by the wayward actions of his forefathers. So, he sought to return to the righteous way of living, and his effort to reignite the family dynasty was to implement—in his oikos—the ways of the family a hundred years before.

In addition to the agricultural commerce and vineyards, the family business eventually included a trucking company. All told, numerous families were dependent upon our family for their day-to-day living. And sadly, most were eking out a pale existence because in South Africa during the 1960s through the 1970s, the day laborers were often paid in part with cheap wine: they were given cheap wine at breakfast, cheap wine at lunch, and a bottle of cheap wine to take home at the end of their shift. This resulted in employers profiting from the clear dependence of their alcoholic employees as few employees were being paid a fair wage for their services. (Tragic, I know!)

Being the close-knit family that we were, the family discussed the grievous way the culture had enslaved its employees and how our family business was complicit. Each had a seat at the table. Views were expressed. With wholehearted family support, my dad intervened: He boldly changed everything the company had done that dishonored God. He began by hiring a teacher. (Actually, a former pastor who was experienced in creating alcohol recovery programs.) He started a community church on the farm. He stopped paying day wages with wine and gave raises to the employees. He and the newly employed teacher walked with employees through withdrawals and aided them toward sobriety. He introduced profit sharing. He founded a farm school for the children of employees and a night school for the employees themselves. And he brought running water and electricity into the homes of many of the local labor force. Many became believers.

As the months progressed and we watched Dad's fervor, we guessed it might take a generation or two for the full effect of these changes to be embraced by all involved and the full blessing of our stewardship to be received. But God! Remarkably, it took less than ten years for the community to be redeemed, for lives to be transformed, and for the people to flourish!

This is what we want—people flourishing! This is the promised outcome of the biblical mandate. And this is what the world needs more of today.

Why Your Family Needs to Be a Dynasty

Earlier in this book, we referenced an article in *The Atlantic* by David Brooks titled *The Nuclear Family Was a Mistake*. His insight into the plight of people is unambiguous. His research and understanding act as a clarion call that should be heeded by Christian families everywhere. Not only because the world needs us to change their lives but because we need to change our own, or we too will flounder. Of the current ways of family in the United States, Brooks says,

> Our culture is oddly stuck. We want stability and rootedness, but also mobility, dynamic capitalism, and the liberty to adopt the lifestyle we choose. We want close families, but not the legal, cultural, and sociological constraints that made them possible. We've seen the wreckage left behind by the collapse of the detached nuclear family. We've seen the rise of opioid addiction, of suicide, of depression, of inequality—all products, in part, of a family structure that is too fragile, and a society that is too detached, disconnected, and distrustful.

His twenty-first-century research reveals what the Bible announced to be true millennia ago. We belong in family. And not just mom and dad, 2.2 kids, furry family pet, and a white picket fence. We belong connected in a trusted network of extended family, who act as a safeguard and a launching pad for the success of the next generation.

But what is the problem of perpetuating the nuclear family? Why is it that small traditional families can't succeed in creating, at a minimum, good citizens and, at maximum, good Christians? To that question, Brooks offers,

> . . . we're likely living through the most rapid change in family structure in human history. The causes are economic, cultural, and institutional all at once. People who grow up in a nuclear family tend to have a more individualistic mind-set than people who grow up in a multigenerational extended clan. People with an individualistic mind-set tend to be less willing to sacrifice self for the sake of the family, and the result is more family disruption. People who grow up in disrupted families have more trouble getting the education they need to have prosperous careers. People who don't have prosperous careers have trouble building stable families, because of financial challenges and other stressors. The children in those families become more isolated and more traumatized.

So, what are you and your family to do? How do you overcome the seemingly inevitable draw toward disconnection and disinterest? How can you impact your church and local community, aiding people in their pursuit of goodness, beauty, and liberty? What is your pathway toward hope and a life-giving, God-glorifying life for you and your family? Here are the seven steps we recommend.

Step 1 – Embrace the dominion mandate as a family

As we started this journey, we began by offering a new way of thinking about the purpose of human existence and the mission of families. But it isn't new. Again, the biblical mandate given to Adam and Eve in the garden is a precursor, if not a foreshadowing, of the Great Commission. They are the same from Adam and Eve to Noah and his sons, then to Abraham, Isaac, and Jacob, and now to you and me—God has been saying you are blessed, and out of that blessing he wants you to enjoy multiplying, filling the earth, and exercising dominion. This is who God has made you to be.

Practically speaking, the shift from a nuclear family to a multigenerational family to an intergenerational family that functions dynastically will begin with one person, or even better, one couple, who believes in God and seeks to trust his plan for their family.

I can imagine that, at this point in the book, you've already started thinking about how to have conversations with your spouse, your parents, or your children about this new way of thinking—that's great! Taken seriously, this will mean a new way of making decisions, and, ultimately, a new way of living. What would it look like if you had monthly family meetings? What would you talk about? How do you approach the conversation of inheritance? What if different members of the family disagree? Is it possible that your prodigal children could come home if you created a place of belonging? Would you have to sacrifice anything now to prepare for the future?

I'll remind you that you don't have to be anxious about today. There is freedom in Christ, and in him, you get to enjoy today—and anticipate tomorrow with hope. As I mentioned before, slow down!

The power is given to your family, so you don't have to do it alone. Likewise, the gifts of the Holy Spirit are given to various members of the body of Christ, the church, so don't go trying to do it on your own. Again, these are the biological and spiritual oikoses working together for the glory of God!

The way we can bring order to the waiting and wanting world is to slow down and create a plan to wield the power God has given to families.

So, think about your family in terms of generations and centuries—not individuals and years. Then you will be able to have the gentle conversations you need to have with your family, inviting them to join you on this slow step-by-step journey of embracing your purpose, identifying your mission, and aligning all of your family's giftings and talents to wield your blessing for the sake of others.

Step 2 – Identify your God-given family name and mission

What is your name? Your parents' names? Their parents' names? As you look forward to future generations, you should look backward and discover your God-given family name and heritage. Just as Trudie and I discovered that land ownership and local commerce are part of our generational heritage, so too are you likely to discover your family workings when you research your family name.

Get connected to your larger family through resources such as ancestry.com or 23andme.com. Find the Hebrew or Greek meanings of your family names. Scour the libraries in your hometown for origin stories so you can understand the lives of your ancestors. Embrace who your family has been—the good and the bad—and trust God to guide you in his faithfulness and to bless your family to the 1,000th generation. Identify your generational blessings and thank God for them!

You will also likely discover that your family has a strong connection to a certain vocation or commitment to a defined group of people. Maybe your great-grandfather and his brothers were all lawyers. Maybe your mom's maternal grandmothers were school teachers. Perhaps you come from a family of business owners, carpenters, or pastors. Or maybe you will discover your family was involved in, for some time, the slave trade, genocide, or organized crime. Whatever you discover, good or bad, trust God with it, talk to him about it, and invite him to re-story your family name so you can embrace your family's dominion rule to be a blessing to others.

This process of discovery can give rise to your family's mandate and help you and your family frame your future. To that end, we encourage all families to discover and define their family mandate and craft a family dynasty statement. And because we believe this is so important, it is the first part of any consulting we conduct with families.

Step 3 – Engage your children and grandchildren with a seat at the table

There is a reason our Jewish friends celebrate their children with bar and bat mitzvahs; this is because, at the age of thirteen for boys and twelve for girls, these family members become adult members of the family—and as adults who are now accountable for their actions. As such, many Jewish families invite their children and grandchildren to share their thoughts and opinions on matters of importance to the family.

When we invite our children to share in meaningful decisions such as moving to a new community, spending or saving money, involvement in church, and hundreds of other topics, we give them a place of belonging, help them envision their future, and train them in the way they should go.

Because so many of our families are separated by geography, busyness, indifference, and societal pressures, it can be difficult to simply be a family, which is what we all want (as we are made to be in a family). No matter the circumstance, by honoring one another with a voice, we foster a trusting environment that makes future conversations and decisions easier.

Additionally, by involving multiple generations at the same time, there is effectiveness that comes as a result. We all know the infamous "telephone game" where one person whispers a phrase to a second person only one time, and that person whispers what they think they heard to a third and so on until the final person sheepishly announces what they think they heard, and everyone laughs at the absurdity of the miscommunication that just occurred. When engaging your children and grandchildren at the table, the elders of the family can effectively make pronouncements, pray, guide, and ask questions with clarity that the whole family understands and can respond to. Again, consider the ways of the British Monarch, who directs all members of their family simultaneously across the generations.

Something to consider is that, according to the Pew Research Center, there has been a resurgence of multigenerational households in the United States in the last twenty years. "The most common type of multigenerational household . . . consists of two adult generations, such as parents and their adult children."[2] If you want to launch your family into a biblical dynasty, engage your children and grandchildren more quickly, grow your capacity to influence faster, and create an environment in which your family can thrive (this might even include living in one household, family compound or even on one street or in one neighborhood).

But please know, the power of a family dynasty is not limited by proximity. Our family dynasty is at work on three continents. And while we don't meet in person at the Family Table as often as the Dewing family does, our communion and fellowship are both strong and constant.

Step 4 – Grow your capacity to exercise dominion

Exercising dominion is about quantity and influence.

In the same way that the most economically viable countries have the most people, the largest families have the greatest capacity for impact. As we have seen, this can be achieved through biology, adoption, or even connecting your family household with others through the local church. The key here is to never go at life alone! Talk to your immediate family members, aunts and uncles, cousins, grandparents, and children, and find ways to grow closer together instead of further apart. And whenever possible, make the business of the family the family business.

Influence is directly related to credibility. What are your circles of influence? What is your family's reputation in that sphere? Do everything you can to be a blessing to others.

Influence is also related to finances. The greatest opportunities for the growth of financial capital are in property ownership, and to a lesser degree, the securing of intellectual property. If needed, seek expert counsel to position yourself as being both free from debt and having a growing capacity to generate income through real estate and other investments. Avoid dividing your family assets through individual inheritances; rather, strategically place them in a consolidated structure, where the family can manage and grow them together.[3]

Step 5 – Create an environment in which each member of your family can thrive

We already know the purpose, strategy, and ultimate victory that each family is a part of. God is blessing the nations by being a blessing to his children. He has given spiritual gifts to individuals, the five-fold ministry to the church, and the capacity to wield dominion to families. In every facet, we are to embrace his calling on our lives to be a part of his kingdom.

God enjoys having a unique relationship with each one of us "for we are God's handiwork, created in Christ Jesus to do good works, which God prepared in advance for us to do" (Ephesians 2:10). In light of our earlier comments about identifying a family mission, we must stress an obvious family history does not demand sameness. Each unique person with their own gifting should be empowered to serve God through the family in a way that honors God, fulfills their calling, and provides for them.

I know of a family of entrepreneurs. From parents to grandparents, siblings, and cousins, nearly all of them at one time or another, have started or owned a small business. Here, members of the family could be invited to work in one of those businesses, be supported in starting their own business, or become a consultant, or a teacher to help other people succeed in business. Or maybe, they will be supported by the family in their effort to become a musician or artist who need a business manager to help them succeed. Whatever the circumstance, each of us should be given the freedom to love God and others with the support of our families.

Step 6 – Take the first step toward reconciling prodigals

Families are where each of us belongs. And there is no doubt the enemy has succeeded in peddling the lie that we do not need family and we can succeed on our own. There is no doubt that sin has caused pain, and family members have become separated, sometimes for good reason. But God has given us the ministry of reconciliation (2 Corinthians 5:18). This is clearly to enable us to be ambassadors for Christ, that people would be reconciled to God, but also to enable us to seek out and reconcile people with one another, and sometimes with us.

I have good friends whose marital affair and subsequent divorce resulted in nearly twenty years of isolation and silence between parents and children. Then, with a heart of contrition and a desire for family restoration, and with a mind toward embracing the capacity God gave them as a family, the patriarch of the family began seeking to reconcile with every child he had grievously pained. It took years, but God's grace and the man's humble faithfulness finally brought the fractured family back together. And they smiled because one of the daughter's husbands worked in the same industry as her father, and he ultimately joined his father-in-law in business.

Prodigal sons and daughters often leave home to find what they need, a place of belonging. When moms and dads create the space for children to know they are loved, believe they belong, and can be a part of something more significant and larger than themselves, they will often come running home. This is the power of creating the family table.

Step 7 – Influence your church and communities

It is within the DNA of every oikos to grow, to be a part of something, and to build something. We should all have the same conviction as Joshua, who chose not to serve himself, not build his own empire, and not seek other gods, saying, "But as for me and my household, we will serve the LORD" (Joshua 24:15).

Churches are a family of families. Communities are a social

construct in which families live and work together. And it is in these two places that you and your family are meant to thrive.

Christian families need to stop church-hopping. Church families need other church families to help them grow and become all that God desires them to be. Children need to see their parents value the body of believers; otherwise, when they leave home for college, they will likely discount the church in the same ways their parents have. This is why fundamental to all of what we've looked at together is the willingness to submit to the authority of God. One way we do this is by persevering our commitment to the church and by submitting to spiritual leadership.

Christian families need to actively engage in our communities, bringing the transforming power of the Gospel with us wherever we go, no matter the sphere of influence. The people who live in every facet of the Seven Mountains (arts and entertainment, business, education, family, government, media, and religion) need the authority of Christ, carried by believers, to reconcile them to God. This is how God's people bless others!

The Louis Family

In the 1980s and early 90s in South Africa, the Louis family bent their knee in worship of God amid civic and religious efforts of the people to bring restoration and healing to a country burdened by the plight of racial hatred and violence.

As members of our church community, Michael Louis and his brothers embraced our efforts to not only protest the apartheid regime but to provide solutions to aid in the transformation of the culture. And what a remarkable effort it was! In partnership with the Heritage Foundation and others in the United States, we hosted community symposiums on the biblical reconstruction of the nation. Supported significantly by the Louis family, these symposiums sowed the seed that led to future events where more than a million

Christians gathered together, crying out to God for the transformation of South Africa.

Acknowledging the will of the people, Michael founded the Christian Democratic Party to be a voice for the people amid changes in the nation. So successful was the political engagement that Nelson Mandela invited Michael to join the team responsible for writing the new South African constitution! Michael is a man after God's own heart and an expert in constitutional law; his fingerprints are readily seen all over the new constitution! It is rich with a biblical worldview and an upholding of natural and moral law.

During the process of writing the formative guiding document for the future of the country, Michael built into the constitution a recognition of liberty at the city level in South Africa. Cities play a profound role in the transformational work of God. (Many believe God began his work in the garden, but he will finish it in the cities.) Much can be said about the government of nations and the capacity to do good for the people, but it is truly at the local level where family dynasties can transform schools and streets, finances and family, poverty, and politics.

Seeking restoration of what was lost during the many years of violence, segregation, and gang warfare, the Louis family set their minds on healing local communities first. In a recent election, they raised and supported nearly a thousand local candidates, with hundreds of them being elected by the people to become mayors and city council members. Not satisfied with having the right people in places of power, the family then created training institutes focusing on governance, stewardship, accountability, and cultural transformation. The Louis family's mission to see families and communities free from the abusive tyranny of regional dictatorship is now liberating people from spiritual, political, and racial bondage.

It should be noted that not everything the family touches turns to gold. During the COVID-19 pandemic, certain aspects of the family's enterprise struggled as commerce waned and travel restrictions reduced business activities. But because members of the family have various talents and interests, the family business investments were sufficiently diversified. Collectively, the Louis Family was able to carry those endeavors hardest hit. This is a key to the strategy of family dynasty—a family can diversify holdings, revenue, and liabilities in a way individuals simply cannot.

Everything the Louis family does is to bless the families of the earth by fostering freedom so families can flourish. Praise be to God for faithful and faith-filled families!

∼

Reflection Questions

1. Every family of faith began with one person, or one couple, believing in God. That faith led to trusting in God and obeying God. Who is that person, or couple, in your family lineage? What's their story?
2. David Brooks of *The Atlantic*, wrote, "We want close families, but not the legal, cultural, and sociological constraints that made them possible." Do you agree with Brooks' assessment? Why or why not?
3. The seven steps to building your family dynasty are life-giving and God-glorifying. Reflect on each step. Which step do you find most exciting? Which one do you find most challenging? Which step do you believe is the most important? Journal your answers.
4. Christian families are needed to actively engage in our communities, bringing the gospel wherever we go, in every cultural facet (arts and entertainment, business, education, family, government, media, and religion). What area(s) do you believe God is calling your family to enter into? Explain.

11
YOUR FAMILY'S MISSION

Their descendants will be known among the nations and their offspring among the peoples. All who see them will acknowledge that they are a people the Lord has blessed.

~ Isaiah 61:9

As I have already shared, my dad was the pivot point for my family's initial embracing of the idea of functioning as a family dynasty. It was our research of the Morris family line that illuminated our understanding of how, at different times, throughout many generations, our family leveraged our land to benefit the community by funding churches, hiring pastors, and employing people.

He was the one who engaged us to contribute to the decision-making on how to run our family business in South Africa. I know I have already shared how my dad's heart for God and love for our neighbors was the catalyst for community-wide transformation in a wine-farming region close to Cape Town, South Africa. But I am so grateful that our family story does not end there.

The House of Morris is Gaining Dominion

Years later, prompted by an unexpected and unsolicited offer to buy our family trucking business, my father determined it was the right time to sell the company. He then led our family into a new endeavor, this time in water parks.

Following a successful season of growing hospitality in the region, my dad was once again presented with an opportunity to sell the business. But before my parents could entertain the thoughts of dispersing the family assets and dividing the inheritance amongst the children, I advocated for a tactical shift that would solidify the future of our dynasty.

With my youngest brother at the helm, we doubled down on our business, and the influence our family wielded in The Strand/Somerset West, a community outside of Cape Town. Once again, not settling for just business success, we spearheaded efforts to impact our community. My dad funded a line item in the company budget dedicated to supporting kids in the community who wanted to go to college. He began a work program for kids who weren't in school to work at the water park, and as they demonstrated effort and a desire to learn, he gave them a pathway back into school and the possibility of earning a college scholarship.

Because of our family's reputation, under the leadership of my brother, the water park now functions as an integral hub for community activity in the region. A few years ago, it was even selected as the agreed-upon neutral, safe place for major rival gang leaders to have reconciliation talks guided by civic leaders. After years of violence, hundreds of lives lost, and untold negative effects on the community, the way we were going about caring for people made it possible for hardened criminals to believe we cared about them as well. They met at our business to talk with officers of the court and government officials to determine a pathway to peace.

Today, we are building upon that identity as a place of healing and belonging. My brother hosts prayer events, community meetings, and weekly marketplace activities that enable entrepreneurs to sell their goods. We also fund local charities that operate out of our facility. And we celebrate the hundreds of kids who have met Jesus, gotten out of the street life, and gone back to school because of God's goodness.

Even our daughters, Sabrina and Amber, are carrying on the family tradition of caring for people while endeavoring in entrepreneurship. (Both now own their own businesses.) Sabrina's enthusiasm for the House of Morris is a huge encouragement to Trudie and me. And Amber's love for working with those with special needs inspires us.

But what is perhaps most amazing is that they are part of a long Morris family value—our two daughters have a seat at our family table because we adopted them many years ago and bestowed upon them the full blessing of our family. And their adoption marked the fourth consecutive generation in which women have been adopted into the Morris family! Praise be to God!

It was just forty years ago that our family business was in transition and was facing financial ruin. Now, because of God's blessing and our empowerment by the Holy Spirit to accept God's call on our family to influence our community, the Morris family dynasty continues to wield dominion on earth. And every Christian family who professes the name of Jesus to the glory of the Father can do the same.

So, let us again turn our attention to your family and how you too can wield family dynasty to take dominion and fulfill your family's God-given mandate.

Christ and Culture

H. Richard Niebuhr's *Christ and Culture* is a foundational read for the contemporary church and Christian families alike. This theological and missiological work penetrated the churches' thinking to such a degree that current writings often build upon it or reference it, including D.A. Carson's *Christ and Culture Revisited* and Tim Keller's *Center Church*.

Starting with basic Christology, or a definition of who Jesus Christ is and the implication thereof for all people, Niebuhr presents a valuable awareness of the tension of living faithfully under the authority of Christ while living in the culture around us. He presents various approaches for the Christian:

- Christ against Culture
- Christ of Culture
- Christ above Culture
    - Both Christ and Culture
    - Christ and Culture in Paradox
    - Christ as Transformer of Culture

If you are not familiar with Niebuhr's approaches, allow me to summarize them for you.

The idea of **Christ against Culture** is a favorite amongst monks, Mennonites, Quakers, and those who would readily reject culture and separate themselves from all worldly endeavors and interests as possible. They view the kingdom of God as being at odds with the kingdom of this world and are committed to living exclusively in the kingdom of God.

The notion of **Christ of Culture** is favored by those who see Jesus as "the great enlightener, the great teacher, the one who directs all men in culture to the attainment of wisdom, moral perfection, and peace" (92). For them, there is no tension because God will mysteriously wash away our sin despite our demand to build and worship our own idols.

And regarding **Christ above Culture**, **Both Christ and Culture** are the synthesis version of Christ above Culture, where we worship God on Sundays and live in the world Monday through Saturday. Perhaps trying to reconcile the creation account in which God deems everything good with the fall of Adam and the origin of sin, holders of this position seek to reconcile the tension by moderating between reason and revelation.

For those who hold **Christ and Culture in Paradox**, there is an irreconcilable strain between Christians and culture as a result of the inevitability of human depravity pervading and corrupting all human efforts. Because, as Niebuhr says, "Grace is in God, and sin is in man" (151), we can only live our lives oscillating between the good and the bad, moment by moment.

The **Christ as Transformer of Culture** position is the one held by those who view Christ as the Lord of all people, whether faithful or not, and see all creation and culture ultimately under the judgment and/or the deliverance of God. By emphasizing the goodness of God, these cultural transformers seek to affirm what is good and transform what is corrupted by sin and selfishness.

So, what are we to do? How now should we live? We have asked this before and believe the answer is the same. From the very beginning, God made it clear how we should live, and it is revealed in the dominion mandate to Adam and Eve, the first family, and by extension, the church and every Christian household. This was echoed to Noah and his sons after the flood when the world was ready to be renewed. And it was perfectly proclaimed by Jesus in the Great Commission, which is worth repeating: "Then Jesus came to them and said, 'All authority in heaven and on earth has been given to me. Therefore, go and make disciples of all nations, baptizing them in the name of the Father and of the Son and of the Holy Spirit, and teaching them to obey everything I have commanded you. And surely I am with you always, to the very end of the age'" (Matthew 28:18-20).

The cry of the Christian heart must be, as Jesus taught us to pray, "your kingdom come, your will be done, on earth as it is in heaven" (Matthew 6:10). I sometimes simply call this God's dream, but it is actually his mandate.

Understandably, many Christians seek to separate themselves from the evils of the world because of its capacity to corrupt the very core of our daily lives.

- We are called to make disciples of Jesus, while the world tells us to follow our hearts.
- We are called into the mysteries of God, while the world tells us to follow science (as if the two don't perfectly coexist).
- We are called to obedience, while the world entices us toward selfishness.

We are to be the ones who are leading the sheep. We are to be the ones teaching our children. We Christians are mandated to serve the people of this world and usher in the breakthrough of God's kingdom.

In his classic book, *Roaring Lambs*, former television executive Bob Briner described the importance of God's people engaging in our world vocationally: "Christians of both competence and commitment are needed to penetrate every area of society, and they need to do it with Christ's command to be salt firmly in mind . . . it is about everyday people doing everyday jobs with a very special goal—that of effectively representing Christ in all areas of society."[1] We do this by creating art that glorifies God, running businesses that are successful and contribute to their community, reporting the news with integrity, delivering truth into political discourse, and making military decisions that positively impact the world.

> *Far too many Christians just fold their hands and pray. And pray we should! But I take issue with the folding of Christian hands when there is work to be done.*

Radio talk show host, political pundit, and brother in Christ, Hugh Hewitt, adds that to have this kind of societal impact for God's Kingdom takes hard work and intentionality: "Success in the world is pretty much a function of discipline and effort. Which, of course, raises the stakes quite high for Christians. Given the condition of the world. And given the stakes that ride on the outcome of individual choices, believers do not really have the option of declining to become generals."[2]

In that same way, the men and women who worked for my dad

are grateful my dad chose to become a general. So am I. (Thanks, Dad!)

Dynasty Leads to Dominion

What's so interesting about how God explains or equips us to understand what the impact of family dynasty looks like is that he does so in light of its influence on the community. Isaiah 65 is a wonderful depiction of the fullness of the lordship of Jesus on earth as it is in heaven. You see, the peace of God does not come from the presence of God but from the lordship of Jesus. It is his sovereign rule in the loving will of the Father that makes it possible for you and me to live in peace, even as we wait for the return of our King. But again, we do not wait idly for the promise of the future kingdom because it is now being realized by the dominion rule of Christian families. We see this in Isaiah 65:17-19. While this is often understood to be a foretelling of the millennium, it is also, and perhaps even more so, a promise of what the kingdom of God will look like here on earth when Christians band together to bless people. When we put on our socioeconomic glasses and read it from the perspective of a transformed community, a city of joy, a city of happiness, we have a clear matrix for what the fruit of the biblical mandate looks like. God gives us a quantitative and qualitative measure-matrix of how we can know the degree his kingdom is impacting a community.

There is a health policy. There is an economic policy. There is governmental policy. There is evidence of justice being realized and education being embraced. There is, in essence, what I simply call God's dream.

God's dream for this community is recorded in Isaiah 65 and echoed by Jesus' teaching on the kingdom: "But seek first his kingdom and his righteousness, and all these things will be given to you as well" (Matthew 6:33). Ultimately, everything we do concerning our families has to be about seeing the manifestation of the kingdom of God here on earth.

The essence of God's kingdom, and his dream enacted, is the inevitable fulfillment of his plan "that at the name of Jesus every knee should bow, in heaven and on earth and under the earth, and every tongue acknowledge that Jesus Christ is Lord, to the glory of God the Father" (Philippians 2:10-11). This is God's dream. It is his vision. But it is no fairytale! There are no glass slippers or pumpkin coaches. Instead, there is a king, and there is a kingdom. Right now, people are living in the kingdom of God who believe they have placed themselves on his throne. Thankfully, we are living in the "year of the Lord's favor" (Luke 4:17-21 and Isaiah 61); thus, we must do everything we can to fight for the souls of the men and women who have not yet submitted to the lordship of Jesus. This is our biblical mandate. It is our great commission. And it is our greatest commandment, one the Power family in South Africa takes very seriously.

The Power Family

The Power family owns and operates the most successful construction consortium in South Africa. They use their success, family wealth, and influence to serve their neighbors both inside the company and in the community as a whole.

Seeing the potential of people and knowing that work is noble, they developed an apprentice program that has trained thousands of unskilled workers in preparation for meaningful work. Mindful of the role Christian family dynasties play in the lives of people in their community, Graham Power led his family's effort to change the legal structure of their companies, forgoing the tax benefits of off-shore holdings, and instead choosing to pay the full measure of taxes to the local government.

But more than being a good corporate neighbor, and developing goodwill in the community, the family is committed to spiritual life change for the people of South Africa. They funded a global prayer movement, spearheaded the evangelization of South Africa, and established multiple Christian charities to bring immediate medical and social aid to the most vulnerable in South Africa.

Moreover, the family is challenging others to follow in their footsteps. They founded Unashamedly Ethical, "a global movement of individuals and organizations guided by a founding vision to transform society by taking a stand for ethics, values, and clean living. The goal of this movement is to develop an unashamedly ethical culture among this generation of leaders and the next."[3]

The Power family, as ambassadors for Christ, are changing the way people think about life, business, Christianity, and most important of all—Jesus. The family's efforts to bring order to the world and redeem the pain of broken men and women enhance their credibility as ministers of the Gospel, making other voices and worldviews in the region seem like nothing more than clanging symbols.

Cultural Christianity vs. Cultural Marxism

The battlefield of faith has changed a myriad of times throughout history. But the tact of our enemy has always been the same: "Did God really say . . . ?" The enemy is a liar. Jesus said of him, "He was a murderer from the beginning, not holding to the truth, for there is no truth in him. When he lies, he speaks his native language, for he is a liar and the father of lies" (John 8:44b). Today, the lie we are facing around the globe is the enticement of the teachings of avowed atheist Karl Marx. If you want to understand the teaching of Marxism, in light of its forbearers and followers, I suggest you read Benjamin Wiker's *10 Books That Screwed Up the World*. In this work, Wiker writes, as many others have, that ideas have consequences. He presents the progressive development of secular humanist thinking, beginning with Niccolo Machiavelli and Rene Descartes in the 1500s, to Karl Mark and Friedrich Engels in the 1800s, and to Margaret Sanger and Adolf Hitler in the 1900s. And he throws in the likes of Charles Darwin, Friedrich Nietzsche, Sigmund Freud, and a few others—fifteen in total—in his effort to connect the anti-Christian thoughts of these self-esteemed leftists.

In the introduction, Wiker writes, "Common sense and a little logic tell us that if ideas have consequences, then it follows that bad ideas have bad consequences. And even more obvious, if bad ideas are written down in books, they are far more durable, infecting generation after generation and increasing the world's wretchedness."[4] Generation after generation, the lies of the world are destroying men and women by the millions. Literally! Wiker continues: "If the *Communist Manifesto* had never been written, a great deal of misery would have been avoided. The same is true of Hitler's *Mein Kampf* and the other books on the list, even when the carnage is sometimes of a more subtle and different sort."[5]

It has been a while since we looked at the premise of this book, which is rooted in the idea that God had a plan when he created humanity: "God blessed them and said to them, 'Be fruitful and increase in number; fill the earth and subdue it . . .'" (Genesis 1:28). If God is the father of truth, if the deceiver is the father of lies, if we are made in the image of God with the capacity (by the dunamis of the Holy Spirit, of course) to take dominion here on earth, why are we not doing it?

Wiker summarizes well the efforts of those who are antagonistic toward God in his conclusion, but he does so most poignantly by quoting the Russian religious philosopher Semyon Frank:

> Sacrificing himself for the sake of an idea, he does not hesitate to sacrifice other people for it. Among his contemporaries he sees merely the victim of the world's evil he dreams of eradicating or the perpetrators of that evil . . . . This feeling of hatred for the enemies of the people forms the concrete and active psychological foundation of his life. Thus, the great love of mankind of the future gives birth to a great hatred for people; the passion for organizing an earthly paradise becomes a passion for destruction.

I contend this is the exact opposite of the will of God. This is the antithesis of what Niebuhr envisions when he talks about the *Christ as Transformer of Culture* position that we earlier summarized as those who view Christ as the Lord and see all creation and culture ultimately under the sovereign rule and judgment (or deliverance) of God. By emphasizing the goodness of God, these cultural transformers seek to affirm what is good and transform what is corrupted by sin and selfishness.

But God.
But Dad.
But Mom.
But Family.
But Dynasty.
But Christians.
But the Church.

It is here, in the midst of a spiritual battle being played out on earth, that the family, supported by the church, can wield its dynasty to take dominion, be ambassadors for Christ, and love their neighbor.

John Stonestreet, president of the Chuck Colson Center, was once asked, "Why should Christians care about the culture? It appears we've lost—we have legalized abortion, gay 'marriage,' unisex bathrooms—so why bother trying to change something that seems unchangeable?"

He answered: "I think we care about culture—not because we're winning or losing but because it's what we're supposed to do as humans."[6]

We are ambassadors for Christ when we lovingly earn the right to tell people about God's love for them. And we take dominion by bringing order to a world being ripped apart by the chaos of the lies of the enemy.

We love our neighbors when we care about the culture in which they live.

You don't have to traverse the globe to do it; you can start right in your city. And you and your family *should* start right in your city.

- Be sure your local church and other families are a part of it. Join the growing City Gospel Movement's[7] effort.
- Raise money for suicide prevention in your local schools.
- Fund addiction recovery programs at your homeless shelter.
- Adopt a city park.
- Support a pregnancy resource center.
- Open a new business and employ a dozen people.

Though, you could travel the globe to share the good news of Jesus Christ, just like Watkin Roberts did more than a century ago.

The Pudaite Family

When the Gospel first came to the Hmar tribe in India in 1910, one of the early converts was Chawnga Pudaite, a young headhunter in training. As more and more of the tribal people became Christians, he saw the need for the Scriptures in their native language. Chawnga prayed that someday he would have a son who would learn to read and write so he could translate the Bible into the Hmar language.

Chawnga had four sons, and he named one of them Rochunga (Ro), whom he led to Christ. It would not be long before Ro would become a renowned speaker and evangelist. In his early years, Ro knew God wanted him to go to school, and at ten years old, despite teasing from his friends, Ro became the first boy from his village to pursue a formal education, but it was not easy—it was a long, dangerous trip.

Six days and ninety-six miles later, through a jungle of tigers, elephants, bears, and man-eating python snakes, Ro arrived safely in the village of Churachandpur and started school. He continued his education in Scotland and then at Wheaton College Graduate School near Chicago, Illinois. During his time in school, Ro worked hard on translating the Bible into his native language. Finally, the job was done. He wrapped up the precious manuscript, mailed it to the printer, and at long last, the Bible arrived in Northeast India.

During his years in college, Ro had met and was communicating with a young lady back in Northeast India. Her name was Lalrimawii, which means "the name of the Lord is a beautiful sound." When his work translating the Bible was finished, Ro went back to India and asked her to be his wife.

After all the work of translating the Bible, Ro and his new wife thought the work God had for them was finished. Little did they know that it had just begun. Ro was asked to head the Indo-Burma Pioneer Mission, which later became the Partnership Mission Society in India. And they continued to spread God's love throughout India.

Even though the Hmar people now had the Bible in their own language, many of them could not read. Ro and Mawii started many village schools, high schools, a college, and even a seminary for their people. Today, the original school (and now the largest of all the schools), located in Churachandpur, has over 3,200 students. Perhaps most amazingly of all, the Hmar people now have one of the highest literacy rates of any people group in all of India!

God also led Ro and Mawii to start churches throughout Northeast India. Over 300 churches are now part of the Evangelical Free Church of India, a denomination they founded. After seeing the tremendous impact the Word of God had on their tribe, they embraced a vision to provide God's Word throughout the world by utilizing the contact information available in phone books and the postal system. Partnership Mission Society became Bibles For The World[8] in 1973. Through Bibles For The World, millions of Bibles were mailed to over one hundred countries.

Today, Bibles For The World is led by the third generation of the Pudaite family, John. His talent for seeking and promoting collaboration puts his family, the Pudaite oikos, in the middle of building God's oikodomé—the larger family of families, the church. And along with mobilizing the efforts of Christian families, churches, and organizations to provide Bibles to people around the globe, they continue to operate a hospital, a seminary, and numerous schools in India. And it began with one man and one family coming to faith in Jesus Christ!

Not many people know the name of Watkin Roberts, the missionary from the UK who arrived in India in 1910 with copies of the Gospel of John translated into the local language, but many people around the world know the dunamis of the spirit of God as a result of this one missionary and the Pudaite family dynasty.

Families are the Key to Overcoming Individualism

One of the great challenges we face today in the American church is individualism. And this is perhaps what family dynasty seeks, more than anything else, to overcome. As David Brooks recognized in his research, and I echo here, the detached nuclear family is creating individuals who are self-absorbed consumers instead of Jesus-abiding champions for people. Cultural apologist S. Michael Craven's insight on these matters is so helpful:

> As Americans, we enter the church with nearly overpowering individualist inclinations. We come with and cling to expectations and demands that are centered on ourselves . . . . We grade the pastor on whether or not he has met *our* needs through his sermon and kept us attentive. We don't humbly submit to one another. We refuse church discipline. We argue, gossip, and divide over inconsequential issues. We attack those outside our traditions . . . . Often our attitudes and actions toward each other are shameful and bring disgrace on the name of Christ—and we frequently do so in the face of an unbelieving world. We simply do not fulfill this essential part of God's mission because we fail to demonstrate the reign of God within this authenticating community.
>
> If we don't get this right, our service will remain indistinguishable from any other, and our proclamation of the risen Christ will appear shallow and without bias. If we want to overcome our culturalized Christianity to worship and serve the King of Kings, we must recover a broader understanding of our mission as Christians in the world . . .

. This we *must* do if we want the world to know whose disciples we really are.[9]

This we must do! God has already done his part and is still doing so. He has created us, blessed us, re-storied us, and given us everything we need to rule the world as princes and princesses of the King of Kings. We have the mandate. We have the strategy. And we know victory is guaranteed.

We have the vehicle through which we can establish dominion—family dynasty. We have the spiritual community in which we can worship and be edified—the church. We have the dunamis of the Holy Spirit dwelling in each of us. What else do we need?

Now is the best time for you and your family to get started in revealing God's love to the world. The world is waiting, so as you go, make disciples by loving God and loving others wherever they are. Do so with great confidence that what God started in the garden, he will finish in the cities. May his kingdom come, and his will be done on earth as it is in heaven.

The restoration of the world begins at home—building your family dynasty!

Reflection Questions

1. The Morris family models their daughters having a seat at the family table. Who have you welcomed to sit at your table to pray about, discuss, and strategize your family's plans? Who would/could you invite in the future?
2. Reflecting on H. Richard Niebuhr's classic book *Christ and Culture*, which approach most resonates with you? Explain.
3. In Matthew 6:10, Jesus taught his followers to pray, "your kingdom come, your will be done, on earth as it is in heaven." This is a prayer and a mandate. How are you practicing both the prayer and God's call to action?

4. Everything we do concerning our families must have the goal of seeing the manifestation of the kingdom of God here on earth. How is your family reaching this goal?
5. There are several ways you can take dominion in your city. (We provided a few suggestions.) Make a list of three or four ways that you can take dominion in your community.

EPILOGUE: A LETTER TO "NONFAMILY" FAMILIES

The Spirit of the Lord is on me,
because he has anointed me
to proclaim good news to the poor.
He has sent me to proclaim freedom for the prisoners
and recovery of sight for the blind,
to set the oppressed free,
to proclaim the year of the Lord's favor.

~ Jesus | Luke 4:18-19

I would venture to say every person who has ever lived has been part of a Cinderella story at one time or another. Now, I don't believe most of us have lived a story filled with princes and princesses and ball gowns and castles. Surely, very few of us have ever ridden in a pumpkin coach or tried on a glass slipper. Instead, I believe it is the beginning of the story—the tragedy—most of us identify with. Like Cinderella, we sometimes feel disconnected and isolated from family and friends. Some of us have lost our parents.

Others feel ignored or belittled by the ones they have. Many of us are familiar with blended families and how they can sometimes give birth to unrestrained sibling rivalry.

While most of us see our lives somewhere between the never-ending scrubbing of the kitchen floor and the evening glamour of a royal ball, my heart breaks because I know some who read this book feel like poor Cinderella, stuck in the mire, never to be released. Maybe you feel like the pain of your divorce will never end. Or your heart aches when you see moms and dads with multiple kids in tow while you long for just one child. I imagine some of you are still in search of your biological parents, while others wonder if their lives would have been better had they never adopted their son or daughter. It burdens my heart deeply to know that you may have no family at all. Yet, far more important than me, is the reality that it burdens the heart of God himself.

Yes, the world is full of pain, but it is also full of joy. Right now, we all live between Jesus' ascension and his future return. Today, we live in what both the prophet Isaiah and Jesus proclaim as "the year of the Lord's favor." Jesus has come to demonstrate his love to you. His ministry is one of blessing and freedom. He is at work giving sight to the blind and breaking the chains of slavery, sin, and death. And he is restoring his brothers and sisters in Christ.

One of the lies of this world (and one you are likely to believe) is that brokenness prevents inclusion. This is not true! It never has been, and in Christ, it never will be. It is no accident you are holding this book and reading this chapter. You might feel alone and like you are the only one in your current circumstance. But you are not. If you are a believer in Christ, you have been redeemed. You have been purchased by the blood of your Savior. And he is your King! You belong to Jesus. No matter what your circumstances, you belong to the King of Kings. You belong in his family.

Many passages of Scripture reveal the heart of God. And there are many ways God expresses himself to us in our time of need. He is our heavenly Father. He is the Good Shepherd. He is King. The Psalmist says God is "a father to the fatherless, a defender of widows, is God in his holy dwelling" (Psalm 68:5). We are often told in the Scriptures to care for orphans and widows. Why them? Because it is really hard for a child who has no parent to believe in a loving father. And it is painful for a woman who has no spouse to believe God is her loving husband. God knows the world is broken. He knows we tend to isolate ourselves to hide our brokenness. But we need not. We who are in Christ belong to him, and we belong in his family—the bride of Christ.

Because you are still reading, I know you are courageous. No matter your life circumstances and the images that arise when you think of your family; your strength is an encouragement to me. I know you have hope for the future, even if you cannot see its fulfillment just yet.

I wonder, is it possible that you are the first in your family to learn of his will for families? Perhaps God has chosen to use you to re-story your family and begin a move toward a family dynasty. Is it possible that the chasm between you and your siblings seems impossible for you to overcome but is only one small step for God to cross? Is it possible that you and your family, whatever your family looks like, are currently being restored by the grace of God?

It is no small thing that Paul, in his letter to the church in Ephesus, explains God's heart for "every family in heaven and on earth" (Ephesians 3:15). The church has often proclaimed its hope for the future when "every nation, tribe, people, and language" will worship God together (Revelation 7:9). But little has been said about how every kind of family will be there. There will be single moms, divorced dads, husbands and wives with no kids, and brothers and sisters with no parents. There will be families who have lived and loved across generations. And there will be the man, standing alone, with no one by his side. But we will all be there together because of God's great love and mercy, for this is the time of the Lord's favor. And while God never plays favorites, you are most assuredly favored by him.

How Then Shall You Live?

If you are still reading this chapter, you may feel as though your family is not even close to being a dynastic family. You might be part of a splintered nuclear family with no connection to another generation. Or somehow, you might have even come to believe the lie that you have no family at all. For those of us who are in Christ, we get to live with him. With his family. But what does that look like?

First and foremost, it is being a part of a spiritual community. If you have not already done so, commit yourself to intentionally engaging with a local church community that preaches the Word of God, salvation in Christ alone, and one that seeks the will of the Holy Spirit. Join a Bible study with fellow believers. Connect your child to a group of Christians. It is in this community, empowered by the Holy Spirit, that you will receive restoration into family and will find the key to rebuilding your own family.

Second, we must all persist in asking for help and receiving the love of others. While the world tells us we need to succeed on our own, God proclaims that we are to succeed in the family—both biological and spiritual. I've seen the fruit of the love of Christ firsthand. Not only in my life but in my parent's house. Allow me to tell you a story about my mom.

Caring for the Widow and for Orphans

My mother trained June to be a mother.

June, a beautiful young woman with autism and Down Syndrome, was abandoned by her single mother and left to fend for herself. The pain of the world tore at her soul. She was abused by a man and left destitute with three little girls. Quietly, behind the scenes, my mom and dad cared for June and her girls. They became part of our family. When no one else was there to remove the bondage of the sin that had been thrust upon them, my parents, especially my mom, intervened to care for June and her precious children. Because of the love of God through the local church and our family, June raised her girls well. She loved well. She gained confidence as she embraced her two places of belonging—she discovered she belonged in a family and to Jesus Christ. She and her girls were part of the House of Morris and members of the spiritual community of Jesus, the church.

June cherished her role as a stay-at-home mom. And despite her early, lowly circumstances, June was able to serve her girls and others well. Her church community blessed her to such a degree that June was able to leave property to her daughters when she died.

God actively pursued June and her daughters. The Author of Creation re-storied June's life and family. He completed his will on earth as it is in heaven. Today, the three girls are thriving. One is a school teacher, another is a librarian, and the third is a stay-at-home parent just like her mom.

Recently, I've been reminded that June was not the only one. My parents and our church family cared for many families throughout the years. And today, I'm still hearing new stories from my mom that reveal the extent to which our family dynasty can bless the people of the earth through our God-given capacity to rule. By God's grace, we are playing a role in helping people be restored. We all know that the God of the Bible is a God of miracles. He is also a God of restoration, which is sometimes the miracle we long for most!

Thoughts for You . . .

I dedicated this book to my dad "who trained me up in the way I should go." Here, I acknowledge my mom, who did the same for my brothers and me, for June and her girls, and many others.

I acknowledge I am writing this book to you. While the pages of this book are about God's plan for families and the church, it is also about his love for you. God dreams that we would all live in his perfect will, in his kingdom, and receive his blessing to be fruitful, multiply, and fill the earth with his glory. Each one of us, because of the work of Christ on the cross and the indwelling of the Holy Spirit, can confidently, but with humility, express our heart for God and others through our service and live intentionally for God's glory.

The God of Abraham, Isaac, Jacob, and Joseph, is the God of the many generations, and through faith in Jesus the God of your family. In the same way that his power is at work throughout the globe, redeeming and restoring humanity, his love is transforming families and churches in your city.

You have your mandate from your Heavenly Father. You have been commissioned by Jesus. And you have been empowered by the Holy Spirit. You and your family have been chosen for such a time as this; the world is waiting for the hope you have to be revealed. Invite God to re-story your life and your family and to bless your family to the 1,000th generation so you can be a blessing to others in the name of Jesus.

> *He is inviting you, no matter what kind of family you have had or have now, to join him in enacting his authority on earth so his will can be done here, now, on earth as it is in heaven.*

Now, I pray this prayer for you: "May the LORD give you increase more and more, You and your children" (Psalm 115:14, NKJV).

Dynasty is your family's mandate.

~

Reflection Questions

1. As a member of God's family, through your faith in Jesus, how might you re-story your family? What do you see as the first step in beginning your family dynasty?
2. Consider the significance of both the biological and spiritual families. Which one has had the greatest impact on your life? Explain.

3. Because of the work of Christ on the cross and the indwelling of the Holy Spirit, believers can express their hearts for God and others through service. We do this to bring God the glory that he is due. Reflect on what serving, to bring God glory, might look like for you. Journal your thoughts and dreams.

APPENDIX

Video Teaching Series

Family Dynasty has produced three video series teaching the following:

1. Introducing the Dynastic Mandate
2. Wealth Creation, Generosity, and Family Engagement
3. Creating Spiritual "Sons and Daughters"

Conferences

Family Dynasty hosts regular retreats throughout the year. These retreats involve numerous Family Dynasty leaders and partners and allow families a full immersion experience in a group setting.

Consulting

Family Dynasty gives families a deeper, more personal training experience with one-, two-, and three-day family summits.

Marketplace Leadership Training

Currently launching in various communities, *Destineers* business groups enable civic, community, and commercial leaders to meet on a bi-weekly basis to learn foundational Biblical truths about business and family.

Live Training

The team travels to churches and other organizations to teach four- and six-session series over a Friday, Saturday, and Sunday schedule.

Books And Other Resources

Family Dynasty is producing a full line of age-appropriate books, eBooks, and audiobooks to resource families. Current plans include five adult books, eBooks, and audiobooks; five young adult books, and five children's books, plus other licensed products.

Visit **familydynasty.co** for more information.

ACKNOWLEDGMENTS

Willem & Agie Van Zyl Family: Thank you for always putting our family first. Dad, I will always be grateful for your courage to forgo promotions with the local police department so you could invest in us kids. Mom, I will always smile because of your work as a beloved school secretary and your care in making me my beautiful wedding dress. You both served well; thanks for modeling hard work, fun, and generosity—these will always be the characteristics of our family dynasty.

Gregory Treat: You have stimulated and challenged my thinking on this critical subject for more than a decade. Your counsel has been key to helping me formulate the teaching series that ultimately became the framework and content for this book! Forever grateful.

Chuck Lawrence: Thank you for not taking "No" for an answer and insisting that I teach a series on Family Dynasty, forcing me to put pen to paper. Trudie and I are humbled by the incredible way you and Jamie, as well as the whole church, embraced us, served us, and continue to bless us!

Terry & Susan Moore: Thank you for being immovable and unchanging in our decades together. You and the faith-filled people at Sojourn Church have loved, celebrated, and supported us financially in ways we could never have anticipated. Your consistent encouragement and support are a huge reason the ministry is flourishing today.

Mat & Janice and the Dewing Family: You were the first family in the US to embrace our Family Dynasty Launch journey as we pivoted toward consulting families. Your trust in Trudie and me, as well as the message, spurs us on. We are amazed you have become partners, investors, and now co-laborers. Most importantly, you are dear friends.

Brad Gruber: Thank you for your faithfulness. You have been a friend and partner, helping the dream of this message become a reality for families around the globe. I value your courage to challenge me to go deeper into God's word and to think pragmatically about how this would and could shape families. Keep doing so: the journey continues.

Joe Baker: Thanks for pushing me beyond my comfort zone in those formation stages. I will never forget when you brought us to Glen Eyrie and suggested (insisted) that we host our first event there! Thank you for helping me give birth to the brand and succinct message it carries today: Family Dynasty.

Dave Sheets: Thank you for your confidence in and commitment to the ministry of Family Dynasty. You and your team at Believers Book Services are invaluable partners. I'm grateful for your companionship and coaching in the early days. You are a true friend.

Rob Bentz: Thank you for your careful scrutiny of this book's theology and ideas, which has helped amplify the message.

Cristina Wright: We are grateful for your thoughtful care in editing the words on the page; you helped craft something worthy of our readers.

ABOUT THE AUTHORS

Sean Morris is a pastor, international speaker, and kingdom entrepreneur. He is the president of Family Dynasty as well as the director of business development USA for the Augment Consulting Group. Originally from South Africa, he has pastored churches and led ministries around the globe, including Austria, Australia, and now the United States. He holds a Doctor of Divinity in Christian Leadership from Promise Christian University. He and his wife, Trudie, live in California.

Trudie Morris is a mom and women's ministry leader around the globe. While leading a church in Austria with her husband, Sean, she led numerous Europe-wide women's church conferences, discipling thousands of women. Moved by the archaic adoption laws in Australia, she ran for Federal Senate in Australia, seeking to bring God's grace into the political climate of that nation.

Marcus Costantino is a business and nonprofit leader, consultant, writing coach, and author. He holds a B.A., in Business from Gordon College. Following five years in sales and marketing in corporate America, he worked seventeen years at the Glen Eyrie Conference Center, a ministry of The Navigators. His literary and writing portfolio includes a US Congressman, an eighteen-year-old political prodigy, and various pastors and non-profit executives. His books include *Igniting Your Influence: 21 Speakers, Coaches, Leaders, and Experts help you write your first Book*; *What's Next? Talking with God about the Rest of Your Life*; *No Lucks Given: Life is hard, but there is hope* (co-authored with celebrity Chef Brother Luck). Marcus and his wife, Trista, live in Colorado.

NOTES

INTRODUCTION

1. William Shakespeare, *As You Like It*, (Cambridge University Press, 2009), act 2, scene 7, line 139.
2. C.S. Lewis, *The Weight of Glory*, (San Francisco: HarperOne, 2001), 45-46.

1. THE ORIGINAL FAMILY PLANNING

1. John Eldredge, *Waking the Dead*, (Nashville: Thomas Nelson, 2006), 166.
2. Or *Seed*. This can rightly be narrowly understood to be a messianic promise of the birth of Jesus. It can also rightly be broadly understood at God's faithfulness to his promise to empower his people to carry his blessing to the nations.
3. Learn more visit: https://sojournchurch.org/
4. It must also be noted that the Moore family are founding partners in this message of family dynasty and generously support our efforts to share the good news of God's mission to redeem and restore families and bring about community transformation in the name of Jesus.

2. THE THREE FAMILIES

1. David Brooks, "The Nuclear Family Was a Mistake." *The Atlantic* (March 2020). https://www.theatlantic.com/magazine/archive/2020/03/the-nuclear-family-was-a-mistake/605536/
2. ibid.
3. Tony Evans, *The Power of God's Names* (Eugene: Harvest House, 2014), 18.
4. Morgan Snyder, *Becoming a King* (Nashville: Thomas Nelson, 2020), 182

3. THE GENESIS OF GOD'S DESIGN AND DOMINION

1. Jonathan White, "Dominion Mandate Scorecard." *Theopolis* (November 14, 2023). https://theopolisinstitute.com/dominion-mandate-scorecard/#5bc5814c-41ee-435e-b8d0-538e273a225a
2. N.T. Wright, *The Case for the Psalms: Why they are essential* (San Francisco: HarperOne, 2013), Kindle.
3. The Hebrew word *erets* is translated here as earth. It is most commonly translated as land and even country and countries. See: https://www.biblehub.com/hebrew/776.htm ()
4. Dr. Christopher J.H. Wright, *The Mission of God's People: A Biblical Theology of the Church's Mission* (Grand Rapids: Zondervan, September 2010).

5. DID GOD REALLY SAY...?

1. C. S. Lewis, *Mere Christianity* (New York: MacMillan, 1960), 120.
2. Charles Perrault, "Cinderella; or, The Little Glass Slipper." (hosted at University of Pittsburgh, October 8, 2003). https://sites.pitt.edu/~dash/perrault06.html
3. Charles Colson, *How Now Shall We Live* (Carol Stream: Tyndale House, November 1, 2004).
4. "ArtPrize," Experience Grand Rapids, https://www.experiencegr.com/events/annual-events/artprize.
5. John Adams, "John Adams on Religion and the Constitution," Online Library of Liberty, https://oll.libertyfund.org/quote/john-adams-religion-constitution.
6. David Barton, *America: To Pray or Not to Pray* (WallBuilders Press, January 1997).

6. FAMILY DYNASTY EXERCISED IS DOMINION ENACTED

1. Learn more at www.heroinethefilm.com.
2. Learn more at www.recoveryboysthefilm.com.
3. Dan Witters, "Provo-Orem, Utah, Leads U.S. Communities in Well-Being," (Washington, D.C.: Gallup, March 25, 2014), https://news.gallup.com/poll/167984/provo-orem-utah-leads-communities.aspx.
4. MarketWatch, "10 most miserable cities in America," MarketWatch, July 27, 2015, https://www.marketwatch.com/story/10-most-miserable-cities-in-america-2014-05-07.
5. Ben Fields, "Mayor unveils riverfront project," Herald-Dispatch, February 17, 2015, https://www.herald-dispatch.com/news/mayor-unveils-riverfront-project/article_a455be76-6678-56fe-b794-bc83304350f2.html
6. Learn more at https://heritagefarmmuseum.com/
7. "Our Story" https://heritagefarmmuseum.com/about/our-story
8. "About" https://heritagefarmmuseum.com/about
9. Learn more at https://pullman-square.com/
10. Fred Pace, "New coalition looks to transform West Virginia's economy," Herald-Dispatch, February 8, 2022, https://www.herald-dispatch.com/news/new-coalition-looks-to-transform-west-virginias-economy/article_2a7124ac-36c4-563e-b0f0-cd41737173cd.html
11. Josephine Mendez, "Netflix documentary shows Huntington in different light," Herald-Dispatch, September 14, 2017, https://www.herald-dispatch.com/news/netflix-documentary-shows-huntington-in-different-light/article_0f1a8515-0619-5455-bb4e-35251b44a0e6.html
12. Amy R. Blankenship, Dissertation: "Small Town Urban Revitalization: The Effect of Pullman Square on Downtown Huntington, West Virginia," Marshall University, January 1, 2008, https://mds.marshall.edu/cgi/viewcontent.cgi?referer=&httpsredir=1&article=1493&context=etd
13. Greg Rosalsky, "The best and worst places to live if you only care about money," NPR, December 14, 2021,
    https://www.npr.org/sections/money/2021/12/14/1063903904/the-best-and-worst-places-to-live-if-you-care-only-about-money
14. Stephen G. Dempster, *Dominion and Dynasty: A theology of the Hebrew Bible* (Downers Grove, IL: Intervarsity Press, 2003), 62.

15. For a deeper understanding of family dynasty and the dominion it leads to, interested readers should examine *Dominion and Dynasty: A theology of the Hebrew Bible*, Stephen G. Dempster makes it clear the dominion mandate is not up to us to fulfill —but it is the work of God himself: "It should be mentioned that God blesses human beings with the ability to multiply and flourish in the earth. They cannot accomplish their dominion mandate without reproducing their kind to help them to do it. In doing this, human beings are not acting independently of God but obeying him and reflecting the divine glory."
16. "God loves cities and Christians should too, says Tim Keller," Christian Today, October 21, 2010,
   https://www.christiantoday.com/article/god.loves.cities.and.christians.should.too.says.tim.keller/26938.htm

7. BIBLICAL FAMILIES

1. Learn more at https://www.biblegateway.com/passage/?search=Ephesians%201&version=NIV
2. Alexandra Sakellariou, "One Of America's Most Expensive Homes Is Selling For $295 Million After Bankruptcy," The Richest, January 14, 2022,
   https://www.therichest.com/luxury-architecture/one-of-americas-most-expensive-homes-is-selling-for-295-million-after-bankruptcy/.
3. Rick McKinley, *A Kingdom Called Desire* (Grand Rapids: Zondervan, 2011), 139.
4. See the book of Titus.
5. Timothy Keller, *The Prodigal God* (Boston: Dutton, 2008), 22-23.
6. Learn more at https://www.beyond-gold.org/
7. Learn more at www.samaritanspurse.org/our-ministry/about-us
8. Learn more at www.annegrahamlotz.org/about-anne-graham-lotz/what-we-believe
9. Learn more at www.billygraham.org

8. FAMILY IS THE VEHICLE FOR GOOD OR BAD

1. Learn more at https://www.hobbylobby.com/about-us/our-story
2. Brian Solomon, "Meet David Green: Hobby Lobby's Biblical Billionaire," Forbes, September 9, 2012, https://www.forbes.com/sites/briansolomon/2012/09/18/david-green-the-biblical-billionaire-backing-the-evangelical-movement/?sh=4a9a9ea45807
3. Learn more at https://www.biblica.com
4. Learn more at https://www.mardel.com/about/mission

9. UNDER THE DOME

1. Edwin Robertson, *Dietrich Bonhoeffer's Meditations on Psalms* (Grand Rapids: Zondervan, August 30, 2005), 14.
2. Ibid, 16-17.
3. Ibid, 17.
4. Steven D. Levitt and Steven J. Dubner, *Freakonomics: A Rogue Economist Explores the Hidden Side of Everything* (New York City: William Marrow, May 1, 2005), https://freakonomics.com/books

5. For those who seek to better understand the beatitudes, consider reading Charles Spurgeon's *The Beatitudes* (New Kensington: Whitaker House, September 27, 2012) or John Stott's *The Beatitudes: Developing Spiritual Character* (Westmont: InterVarsity Press, June 2, 2020).

10. DYNASTIC FAMILY BY DESIGN

1. Michael S. Craven, *Uncompromised Faith: Overcoming our Culturalized Christianity* (Colorado Springs: NavPress, 2009), 19.
2. D'Vera Cohn and Jeffrey S. Passel, "A record 64 million Americans live in multi-generational households," Pew Research Center, April 5, 2018,
   https://www.pewresearch.org/fact-tank/2018/04/05/a-record-64-million-americans-live-in-multigenerational-households/
3. In addition to shaping the vision and mission of Family Dynasty, our co-author Gregory Treat provides technical expertise in this area.

11. YOUR FAMILY'S MISSION

1. Bob Briner, *Roaring Lambs* (Grand Rapids: Zondervan, January 1, 1993), 49.
2. Hugh Hewitt, *In, But Not Of: A Guide to Christian Ambition* (Nashville: Thomas Nelson, 2010), 6.
3. Learn more at https://unashamedlyethical.com
4. Ben Wiker, *10 Books That Screwed Up the World* (Washington, D.C.: Regnery, April 15, 2008), 2.
5. Ibid, 2.
6. John Biver, "SPOTLIGHT: John Stonestreet on our Cultural Revolution," Illinois Family Action, May 2018,
   https://illinoisfamilyaction.org/2018/05/spotlight-john-stonestreet-on-our-cultural-revolution/
7. Learn more at https://citygospelmovements.org/
8. Adapted from the Bibles For The World website with permission: https://biblesfortheworld.org/about-us/
9. Michael S. Craven, *Uncompromised Faith: Overcoming our Culturalized Christianity* (Colorado Springs: NavPress, 2009), 200-201.

www.ingramcontent.com/pod-product-compliance
Lightning Source LLC
Chambersburg PA
CBHW072004290426
44109CB00018B/2123